Night Raiders of the Air

Night Raiders of the Air

Being the experiences of a night flying pilot, who raided Hunland on many dark nights during the War

A. R. Kingsford

Greenhill Books

This edition of *Night Raiders of the Air*
first published 1988 by Greenhill Books,
Lionel Leventhal Limited, Park House,
1 Russell Gardens, London NW11 9NN

British Library Cataloguing in Publication Data
Kingsford, A. R. (Alfred Reginald), 1891–1987
Night Raiders of the Air: Being the Experiences of
a Night Flying Pilot from New Zealand who raided
Hunland on Many Dark Nights during the War.
(Vintage Aviation Library 20)
1. World War 1. Air operations by Great Britain.
Royal Flying Corps. Squadron No. 100. Biographies.
Rn: Alfred Reginald Bellingham-Kingsford
I. Title II. Series 940.4'4941'0924

ISBN 1–85367–008–I Hardcover
ISBN 1–85367–009–X Paperback

Publishing History
Night Raiders of the Air was first published in 1930
(John Hamilton Ltd) and is reproduced now exactly as the original
edition, complete and unabridged, with the addition of extra
illustrations and a biographical note about the author.
We are grateful to the author's son, Hugh Kingsford,
for kindly providing these additional illustrations
and information for the biographical note.

Greenhill Books
welcome readers' suggestions for books that might be
added to this Series. Please write to us if there are
titles which you would like to recommend.

Printed by Antony Rowe Limited,
Chippenham, Wiltshire

THIS BOOK

IS

DEDICATED TO MY FLYING COMRADES

WHO

"FAILED TO RETURN."

My thanks are due to Major Gordon Burge, O.B.E., for certain data, which have been obtained from his record—Annals of 100 Squadron.

Nelson,
New Zealand.

CONTENTS

LIST OF ILLUSTRATIONS

Appearing between pages 88 and 89

PROLOGUE

UNDER the humid heat of a tropical sun, the old troopship was steaming her way across the Indian Ocean in the direction of Aden.

Fifteen hundred men were aboard. The flower of the country from which they had sailed, men from Southern seas and of varied callings in life, eager to enter into the fray, side by side with the men of the Motherland.

There was not a breath of wind, the heat was stifling and the men lay about all over the decks, mostly clad in a singlet and shorts. Some were enjoying a game of cards in the welcome shade of the awning, some read, while others were leaning over the rails, watching the calm, almost rippleless sea. Even the sharp bow of the ship hardly disturbed the smoothness of the oily waters.

Away down below, in the bowels of the ship, two men, stripped to the waist, with the sweat pouring off them, were shovelling coal from the bunkers. To look at them, one would have thought they had been at it all their lives. They certainly handled the shovels all right and the black grime of the coal disguised them, yet not three months before, these two men were in civil life, one a school teacher, the other an artist. They had known each other since schooldays and had offered themselves for service. They were ready to do their bit, and on this day, with others, were giving the stokers a spell for an hour or two.

Taken out of the groove, in which the humdrum and routine of civil life had buried them, these two men found things very different in the life of a recruit aboard ship. Drills, parades, orders, everything seemed to be orders, then the stinking mess room, the food, curry and rice, rice and prunes, day after day; bah! who could eat the muck!

Eight bells sounded and up the steel ladders from the inferno below came these two men, glad to greet the fresh air again. They made straight for the canteen, purchased a tin of pineapple, went to a shady corner and devoured it.

"Well, that's a hell of a game," said the artist.

"You're right," replied the other, "still, it's all in the day's work. At any rate you get a variety of jobs at this soldiering," he went on.

"True," was the reply. "It's a change from drill, I hate that. I'm getting out of this outfit as soon as I get a chance."

"What are you going to do?" inquired the teacher.

"Well, I've got a kink I want to fly and I'm going to give it a pop," he said.

"Yes, and break your bally neck," replied the other.

"Might as well do that as be pipped off by one of Fritz's bullets, I suppose," the artist replied.

"You're not game," said the teacher, with a sarcastic grin.

"What's the betting?"

"Well, I won't bet, but you'll be lucky if you ever get in a flying machine, let alone fly one," he added, with still more sarcasm.

"Well, we'll see," said the artist. With this he picked himself up, slung the empty fruit tin overboard and went below.

We leave him to tell you his own story.

CHAPTER I

TORPEDOED

AT an aerodrome, on the corner of the desert, not far from Heliopolis, I saw an aeroplane for the first time, and a queer looking object it was; a network of bamboo with a couple of men in front of the engine, the whole suspended between what was apparently the planes.

This queer object was running along the ground; Rooty, my pal, and I, were all eyes.

"So that's an aeroplane," said Rooty.

"Gee, it's a queer-looking affair," I grunted.

"What's wrong with it?" said a voice behind us. Turning, we saw a real live airman; at least, we concluded so, for he was all dressed up fit to kill. On his head was a huge helmet affair, to serve as a bumper in case of crashes, he explained. A light oilskin suit arrangement covered the remainder of his anatomy, to say nothing of the gloves, with gauntlets nearly up to his elbows. Around his waist was a belt with a big pistol tucked in it and numerous cartridges. He was certainly an airman, for he informed us that he had just returned from bombing the enemy.

The bamboo affair was a Maurice Farman Shorthorn, so the airman told us. Rooty showed his ignorance by inquiring if it really did fly. Of course it would fly; it had been known to reach a height of five thousand feet, could carry two men at once, and bombs, which were thrown overboard in the hopes of hitting the enemy or something belonging to him.

"What about the armoury?" says Rooty, pointing to his belt.

"You mean the pistol?" queried the airman.

"Yep!"

"Ah! to pot the enemy airman with," he replied.

"Lor! Some shooter this feller," thought I, "this must be some sport, potting at one another in the air!"

This sport, as I considered it, impressed me; I would certainly have to give it a pop at once. Yes, an airman I would be, some big game hunting this, great fun dropping bombs overboard and potting at some other bird in the air with a pistol.

Next morning I appeared at the orderly room with the request for an Army form X.Y.Z. Duly filled, I handed it to the Adjutant, who, with an inquiring look, asked:

"Tired of life?"

I assured him "No."

"Well, what the hell do you want to transfer to the Flying Corps for?"

"I don't know, but I want to fly one of those bamboo affairs," muttered I.

At any rate, the long and short of it was that there was nothing doing. No, I was a Lance-Jack,

and I was told straight out that Britain would lose
the War if I transferred. He couldn't lose any of
his trained men and that was all about it.

"Get out of here and do some work," he growled.
I about turned, cursed and got out, determined
to try again at an early date. I'd got the bug.
Eventually I joined the Flying Corps, but much
happened before that.

Aboard an old trans-Atlantic cattle boat as
troopship, late in '15, we crawled out of Alexandria
under sealed orders. Perhaps to Gallipoli, France,
Servia. It turned out to be the last named.

We were well loaded, artillery, six hundred
mules and goodness knows what else. She was
some ship—we chugged along at nine knots or so
for a few days, and all went well until about the
time we were supposed to reach port. I'd been
wanting something to happen for a long time, and
then it came!

Our bad luck started the night before, when
three of us groped our way in the darkness, to get
away from the mob, down among the mules, to
indulge in a couple of bottles of beer, which Smithy
had pinched from the officers' saloon. Smithy fell
down the gangway and smashed one bottle to the
sounds of sweet music, while I, just as big a mug,
after collecting Smithy, stood the other bottle down
while we shared out the remainder of a chicken
also cribbed from the officers' mess. The ship
lurched, over went the bottle and rolled gaily away
among the mules. Matches, struck at the risk of
court-martial, were of no avail, and our thirst was

unquenchable. Jacko, the third member of our party, who had been silent up till this point, suddenly burst forth with a flow of language that— well that'll do. He'd been a tram conductor—bad luck? Too right it was, but then War is War.

And then the big happening—only a few hours from our destination, a black object was seen sticking up out of the water some three hundred yards away. It looked like a pole, whether anyone realised what it was, I couldn't say, I know I didn't. Suddenly there was a terrific explosion, the old troopship trembled from end to end and took a violent list to starboard. Old Tim Heke, the Maori member of our crowd, who was next to me waiting outside the orderly room, yelled "Torpedoed!" Then I realised that something really had happened and that the 'pole' business was of course the periscope. The chappie who fired the shot was not too bad at sighting either—just afore the bridge he got us.

"Every man for himself," was the order, and there were some six hundred of us. Our emergency station was the bow and the great point was to get my lifebelt from there. Rushing around the high side, I found the passage blocked with crowds lowering the boats. Finding it impossible to pass, I doubled back to the starboard side, now under water, and with a struggle, reckoned I could get round. At any rate, I grabbed the rails, and up to my knees in water, with difficulty kept my feet on the slippery deck and gained the other end. Here the first man I saw was my old O.C., who grasped my hand and wished me luck. We had been together away back in early camp days; we knew each other's thoughts and vaguely wondered if we'd meet again.

The 'list' was increasing; how long would she float? Shouts for help were coming from the hold; some poor devils were trapped, the stairs having been blown away, and they were up to their knees in water.

"For Christ's sake, give us a hand, mate!" one yelled, "throw a rope down." It was grabbed before it could be tied, but someone eventually managed to secure it to a winch. One after another, up they climbed, their faces ashened by the terrible thoughts crammed into those few ghastly seconds. They all got safely to the top, except one; he was a bit of a boy; the torpedo had got him, but then, Youth and War march hand in hand.

Rafts were thrown overboard, and men now half-clad leapt into the sea, but before they could reach the top again, the rafts had drifted away. Those precious rafts! No one was able to take advantage of their safety. I watched poor old 'Nic' (he couldn't swim) try to scramble aboard one of them. After a lot of difficulty he managed it and fell, face downwards, legs and arms outstretched like a letter X. But the raft was rapidly drifting in towards the half-upturned hull of the sinking ship. Above they were endeavouring to lower more boats, a difficult job with such a 'list,' and they couldn't see that speck of a raft with one poor kid, half dead, sprawled across it. Down came the boat, laden with anxious souls, and nearer to the spot where it was destined to touch water, that speck drifted. Lower and lower came the boat while that damned raft literally seemed to wait for it. I wanted to shout, "For God's sake, Nic, look out!" but my tongue clove to my mouth, and then it happened. There was no crash, it just descended on him, the raft overturned and I saw him go under, my last sight of the lad.

Again, horror-stricken, I watched them trying to lower a boat full of nurses. Yes, there were some nurses on this old boat, why, goodness knows. No one could blame the Hun for sinking a troopship, but you could blame the transport official who ordered these heroic women to travel on one. Watching the boat trying to descend, one felt something terrible would happen. At first the ropes seemed to jam, it wouldn't move, then it began spasmodically to lower, very slowly, until suddenly the aft davit rope snapped. Bodies were hurled through the air, hitting the water with terrific force. There dangled the empty lifeboat, and beneath it, a struggling mass of humanity, from which muffled cries for help could be heard, help which no one could render.

We threw over a couple of rafts, and eager hands grabbed the one that drifted towards them. It seemed of little avail, as the poor beggars were dragged down by their heavy winter clothing. It was a cold season and the water like ice.

All around now was a scene of confusion,

struggling masses in the water, rafts drifting where they would, some overloaded, others with only one in possession. Only two boats seemed to have got clear away and were some distance from the ship; they were picking up more survivors until they were over full, and around the stern of one, a whole crowd was hanging; it looked as though they must bring disaster to it. Around the old ship was a mass of dangling ropes where the boats had been lowered. Then the latrines at the stern end fell overboard and the whole collapsed as it hit the water, mercifully making improvised rafts for those who could avail themselves of them. One humorist drifted gaily by, supported by a seat with the familiar oval shape as a lifebelt. Fate had certainly been kind to him.

A yell from the bridge, "Everybody overboard!" reminded me that I was not. The old ship gave another lurch and began to settle down. The rails on the starboard side were well under water and it was certainly time to quit. I didn't even possess a lifebelt, mine had gone; those swines of Dagoes, there were six of 'em aboard, had pinched a whole bunch, tied them together and jumped for it. Four of them were drowned and they damned well deserved it.

Looking round, I spotted a belt tied to the rails now under water, and sliding down into the wet, I found that the infernal tape had expanded and wouldn't come undone. She'd sink before I could get it—I was getting windy and came out in a cold sweat. It looked as though this was the end of it—she was sure going. Something seemed to whisper "Get overboard boy, don't wait!" so over I went, my uppermost thought being to get away from the ship before she took her final plunge. I was still windy, a horror of being sucked down with her possessing me, but how to get away? Heavy boots, clothing, a mass of wreckage and those darned dangling ropes made it difficult to swim; this was the end, no one could get out of this. I seemed to lose heart, terror and exhaustion were gaining hold upon me; looking up, I saw the funnel directly above me; it couldn't be long now, she was sinking fast. Then I spotted a raft, only a few yards away, there were several fellows hanging on to it, and I made a desperate effort and reached it. Once at the raft I discarded my heavy outer garments and boots in case I had to swim.

The old ship had not gone yet. She was still there standing nearly vertical, stern towering a couple of hundred feet above the water. We were some distance from her now, drifting with the tide, and silhouetted against the sky could be seen the figures of some men still on board. What on earth were they doing there?

"Get off, you fools," we wanted to yell, but they'd left it too late, she was sinking fast. There was a terrible crashing in the bowels of the ship and down, down she went, her aft mast disappearing. Only her stern left now; one of the fellows on the stern jumped; we knew what his fate must be, and then she disappeared completely, almost without a sound, save for the swish of the waters as they closed over her.

So the old troopship went, leaving those of us who had survived, dotted about on the high seas.

And all this happened in thirteen minutes.

. . . . .

Many of those heroic nurses were among the one hundred and forty-nine reported 'Killed.'

CHAPTER II

AFTER

ON waking next morning, I had not the slightest idea where I was—there were sheets on the bed and my first thought was home! Gosh! it was some cosy bed: I hadn't slept in sheets for a year or more and I was tempted to turn over when a cheery voice said:

"Well, and how are you?"

Realising it was a woman's voice too, I was roused to a point of interest and opened my eyes. MY! What a picture presented itself: I was looking up into the most perfect sight I'd ever seen, a nurse, and a pretty one too.

She wanted to know how my chest felt.

"Chest, what's the matter with my chest?"

Then I took a deep breath, "Cripes! Well I don't know, but it feels as though someone's sitting on it." Something was wrong, and then I remembered, the rough sea, the hanging on with my arms over the raft, water up to my neck, and how the waves incessantly banged my chest against the wood. It was like raw meat, but I hadn't felt it till now. But what did that matter, I was alive; my mind then wandered back through the past day's events, the torpedo, those hours drifting about in the icy water, the cheering when those three Greek boats appeared, and the cursing and oaths when they passed us by, taking no notice.

Until then our spirits were high, but the increasing roughness of the sea and the driving rain only added to our discomfort. Then that mere slip of a boy on our raft, half-frozen and seasick —we were all getting like that—who begged us to let him drown. Poor devil, we were getting into that state ourselves, floating helplessly about at the mercy of the waves and the rapidly approaching darkness. Our outlook certainly was bad and we wondered what was the best thing to do, hang on, or just slip quietly off and finish it. The night— no one could stick it—we would all be dead by morning—but hang on boy, while there's life there's hope. Just then an object floated past, a man with a lifebelt on, head back and obviously in a state of dead exhaustion; yes, that's how we'd be in the morning, and already darkness was fast approaching.

Then, ah! then Providence acted. No one knew from whence it came and there was no cheering, we'd all got past that, but there, right on top of us was a ship, two in fact, steering slowly between the rafts and specks of humanity in the water. Fellows were already being hauled up the rope ladders: my God! we were saved. What an experience though. Yes, I remembered everything, the rescue boat, those Jack Tars, the feed they gave us. Shall I ever forget how good that chicken broth tasted and how many bowls of it I devoured. Yes, it was good to be alive. Then later, the sailors' clothes and our trying to get into them, the hospital ship and the bed with sheets.

A few days of life on board the hospital ship and we were fairly right. We were all examined and a number were told that they would have to return to Egypt and light duty for a bit. Poor old Claude was bad, got crushed somehow, both legs and chest, he only lasted three days.

We were loath to leave this ideal abode but after about a week living like lords, we were discharged as fit, and it came as a terrible shock! They tried to equip us from the ship's quartermaster's store, for we had lost everything, and I, for one, was rescued in shirt and pants.

When we marched ashore at Salonika, it would have been hard to find a more comical looking crowd.

Leading out of Salonika, there are two roads in a northerly direction, one to Monaster and the other being the Doiran Road. Our new home, so we understood, was some eight miles up the Doiran Road. We would see the tents on the right, so they told us, and we set off with our hopes running high, although some were still feeling pretty rotten. Most of us had colds, to say nothing of rheumatics, sores, etc. For some five miles or so we trudged on, Sergeant Fritz in command, when someone got a hunch that we were on the wrong road. As it happened, he was right, and bad language ensued —Sergeant Fritz was a bloody fool, we were all unanimous about that; anyway, we were Bill Massey's tourists, so why worry.

Motor lorries were moving up and down and there was plenty of transport. We climbed on to some of them and went back to have another look at Salonika. We couldn't take the wrong road this time, and once again set off. We found the thoroughfare a very busy one, with great activity generally, troops, artillery and transport. But what a queer looking lot the troops seemed. They apparently trotted along any old how and all over the show, some leading mules with no bridles or harness, and all very poorly clad, some even having no boots, just old sacking tied round their legs. And their uniform, if one could call it such, was patchy and odd and no two seemed to be alike. We were informed that this was the Greek Army, and the only conclusion we could come to was that they must all have been torpedoed the same as us: at least that is what their appearance conveyed.

Eight miles up this road, we halted to see if any unoccupied tents were in sight. There was a big French camp on our left, and as we'd had nothing since leaving the old mill and were feeling mighty hungry, we strolled over and found the Froggies hospitality itself. Yes, they'd heard about a boat being torpedoed—have a feed? Of course we would, that's what we'd come over for.

They informed us that a big British camp was just started a little further on, so, greatly refreshed, we trudged on again for another half-hour or so, when we found our cook and his staff, who had preceded us, preparing a meal of bully beef and biscuits by the roadside. Being still hungry, we fell to, but where was the camp?

A red-tabbed Johnny had told the cook that this was the site for our camp and that the tents were coming up, so there was nothing for it but to wait. It was night when the tents arrived and we were all huddled together and shivering with cold. Realising that this was to be our base for the present, we set to and pitched the tents, but were not sure that it didn't look even less cheerful than the old mill we had left that morning.

Days in this camp, away out from Salonika, were very dreary and uninteresting. There was little, if any, fighting going on in this part and there were very few casualties coming down. With an hour's physical jerks to commence the day, route marches and drills were the orders. We got the camp pretty ship-shape, more troops arrived and the camp grew larger.

It was this growth of the camp that more or less caused our peaceful life to be suddenly disturbed. One peaceful morning, high up in the sky, someone spotted an aeroplane, flying round like a great silver bird with the sunlight playing on its wings. We were full of interest, although it was too high for us to determine whether it was an enemy machine or not, and we were not familiar with any clues for recognising them. Any doubts we might have had were quickly dispelled, however, and a buzzing noise could then be heard as though something was spinning round. It came nearer,

nearer, louder and louder and was almost over our heads. We ducked instinctively, just in time—bang!—there was a terrific explosion and earth went hurling through the air in all directions. The bomb had hit not fifty yards from where we were standing and struck a bank where a camp had recently been evacuated. At the time it was covered with black crows, scavengers who always helped to clear up the camps, but the bomb scattered them and dead crows were lying about everywhere.

The Hun, flying a Taube, had registered a direct hit on these crows, and the second bomb, descending just behind our camp, did less damage. Then we heard the guns on the battleships in harbour open up and saw tiny flecks of white cloud appear very close to that small silver speck in the sky, which soon disappeared as quickly as it had come.

That was my first sight of an enemy machine and I wasn't too keen on standing on the ground to be potted at from above. I wanted to be up there, and that reminded me, now that we were getting settled down I would renew my application for transfer into this flying business. Approaching my Orderly Sergeant, however, he advised me to wait a bit; no chance of it while we were in Greece, but we were not likely to be there long, so he said.

The following morning, that cheeky Hun showed up again at about the same time, the same silver speck, high up in the clouds. As soon as he got overhead, he started to unload, and his first bomb blew up the bakery just down the hill, killing Sergeant Don and three of his men. The whole show was blown to bits. Certainly these bombs did things properly. These raids gave one an uncanny feeling and I didn't know what to make of them. The same machine continued its bomb dropping, day after day, and then went back the same way as it came.

After this, we formed a working bee and everyone set to work to build dug-outs, taking to picks and shovels for exercise. Running times improved too, and I'm sure Rooty lowered his record the morning a bomb landed forty yards or so from the tent he was in. He literally flew, and we were all like a lot of rabbits running to our holes when the raids started. It was amazing how many men could cram themselves into such a small space.

The last one in, or partly in, was unlucky, as it fell to his lot to poke his head out occasionally to find where the infernal machine was. We could hear the drone of the engine, out would go the head, then in again "toute suite," "He's right overhead." Everyone would hold their breath and shut their eyes, then wonk! another bomb dropped, but we were still alive. He couldn't have many more left now—have another look—good, he's off home. Out we would come, the last man usually gasping for breath, after having been nearly suffocated.

This state of affairs went on for some time, until a few British machines appeared on the scene and we got a little peace, until one night, when we had

turned in as usual and the camp slept, we heard a
terrific explosion just about midnight. It seemed
as though the whole earth shook, everyone jumped
up and I poked my head out of the tent door, to
see a perfect moonlit night and hear the drone of
an engine. In fact there seemed to be more than
one and I scanned the sky until I could locate the
row.

"Look here, boys," I yelled, "it's a damned
Zepp."

Sure enough it was. "Look out, bob down."
We could hear the now familiar spinning noise, a
bomb, and we were only half-way to our dug-out
when it exploded. Some fell flat on their bellies,
while others doubled back into the tents. It was
a nightmare all right, then the Zepp left us and
went on to Salonika, unloading some nine or ten
bombs on the town and doing considerable damage.
I think he was trying to get those battleships in the
harbour. They were certainly trying to get him
and kicked up an infernal row between them.
Smithy and I decided that this blasted place was
no good, bombs by night and bombs by day, hell of
a hole.

After a while, we became quite accustomed to
these raids, although it seemed almost obvious that
they couldn't hit us. They'd tried hard enough
anyhow, and we all had souvenirs, caps of bombs
or other parts. Eventually we became quite brave
and even stood at the tent doors to watch the raids
instead of doubling off to the dug-outs.

Then one night we were treated to a thrill. The

Zepp had paid its usual visit and was over the harbour. Searchlights were flashed on, and although some ten miles away, we could plainly see the silvery outline of the Zepp from where we were. Guns were busy and the enemy was having a hot time, shells bursting all round him and some dangerously near. He unloaded his bombs, apparently all together, for there was a succession of explosions. He had his nose up in an endeavour to climb, but the searchlights still held him and he couldn't get out of it. Soon they'd hit him, surely, there must have been a dozen guns going all out.

At last they got him, and that silvery looking object burst into flames, illuminating, as it seemed, the whole heavens. It began to fall, very slowly, then faster, until, a blazing inferno, it burst in two. The whole countryside was lit up, and down she went into the marshland below. We watched her, still burning, and then, when all was quiet, we crept back into our tents and slept.

After this we enjoyed a period without raids from the enemy airmen and things in general seemed somewhat improved, save for the weather.

CHAPTER III

WE MOVE AND MOVE

GOOD news! we are to quit this show. Everybody is happy, and can you wonder at it? for life had been pretty cheerless in Greece. It is a most uninteresting country and Salonika is a dirty, filthy hole. There always seemed a lot of worshipping and praying going on, but it didn't make them clean. The sanitation was rotten, streets never swept, we wondered they didn't all get fever and die.

As we were soon to say "Cheerio," I was bundled off with orders to the A.M.L.O. and found him in a billet, not far from the bird cage. Tony, one of our hard affairs, who had done more field punishment (No. 1) than all the rest of the crowd put together, was in the clink, so I popped round to see him. There he was, still merry and bright, nothing worried Tony, his only trouble was his shortage of gaspers. The bird cage was the usual thing, barb wired up to about twelve feet and divided with squares of about twelve yards or so, with bell tents for the prisoners to sleep in and a strong armed guard at each of the exits.

In the next square to Tony, seated on a box at

the tent door, was an old Turk, wearing a red fez.
He was the picture of abject misery, hands clasped
together, he sat perfectly still and gazed straight
ahead.

"Who's the cheerful looking soul inside?" I asked
the guard, feeling interested.

"You'd look cheerful, too, mate, if you were in
his place," he replied.

"Oh! what's he been up to?" I inquired.

"Spy," he whispered, "going to be shot."

"When?" I asked.

"After dinner in the square," he replied, "going
to make an example of him."

Poor old devil, I thought, having another look
at him, but still, a spy's a spy, and he knows the
penalty if caught.

Eaten up with curiosity, I hung about until after
dinner and found myself walking towards the
square. I'd seen men shot before, but not this
way, I must see this.

Arriving at the square, I found that a crowd
had congregated and it was impossible to get near.
I accordingly scaled the nearest lamp post and
made that my grand stand. Only just in time too,
for the firing party was already there, about a
dozen of them.

The crowd was babbling away, with mixed excitement, then all was hushed and everyone craned
their necks. I could see the figure of the Turk
approaching and noticed he could hardly walk, the
guards on either side keeping him supported. What
a horrible stillness there was, someone sniffed, one

or two coughed, and women pulled out handkerchiefs.

They stuck the huddled figure against the wall,
quickly blindfolded him and tied his hands behind
his back. An order was given, the crack of the
rifles, the huddled figure sank to the ground, and
the penalty was paid. There was the example. I
shuddered and hurried from the scene: it haunted
me for days.

The trip back to Alexandria only took four days
and we were much relieved. We steamed into the
harbour with vivid recollections of our last sea
voyage uppermost in our minds. Submarines were
still active in that part, but things in general were
much better organised, boat drill, plenty of escorts
and even the troopship boasted guns.

From Alexandria we journeyed to Ismalia and
here found the first Anzac Division remobilising
prior to going to France. It was good to be back
with our Maoriland brothers.

After the intense cold of Greece, the warmth of
the desert was very welcome, our only trouble
being thirst. Yes, we could raise a thirst all right.
We'd line up in the morning and get our water
bottles filled to last us through the day, and then
in the evening you'd find one acting barman in the
tent on the corner of the camp. We had a barrel
of beer there. A fresh one was sent up every morning
and without fail there'd be a queue waiting at
seven p.m., and no one left that tent until the barrel
was empty. It was always well tipped too, just to
make sure there was none left.

After a short stay we packed up and got out, left the desert, trained back to Alexandria and sailed for 'Somewhere in France.'

We were all speculating; rumour had it that we were not going to France, but to Hornchurch, the New Zealanders' Camp in the Old Dart. It seemed too good to be true and a spot of leave would go well, not that we'd done anything to warrant it, nevertheless we would not refuse it. Excitement ran high, especially when we began to steam up the Channel, with land in sight on both sides. The question was, which side would we steer for? Jove! I hadn't seen the old country for years, the last I remembered being a glimpse of Plymouth and then the old lighthouse disappearing in a fog, and here we were now, only the matter of a few miles away.

Slowly we ploughed our way up the Channel. It was now mid-day, Cook-house was sounded, but hardly anyone went down, they were all too jolly excited. It certainly looked as though we were getting a bit nearer to the left side, the coast line now being quite plain. Looking over to the right, that strip of land had about disappeared and it really looked as though we were making for Blighty.

Only a short time elapsed, however, and there didn't seem much doubt. We were making for an opening in the coast line and there was apparently another a little farther down. Mirf reckoned the bit of land between those two openings was an island, and Rooty, whose geography had not been neglected, tried to figure things out. His calculations found that the bit of land with the green grass must be the Isle of Wight and we were making for Southampton. The green grass became nearer, we were only a mile or so away, there were houses too. Now we were passing up a channel with beautiful country on both sides, passing several ships coming out.

After the monotonous sand of the desert, this rich green of the countryside was delightfully refreshing to our eyes, and I literally feasted upon it. The month of June found England at its best, and the picture presented to us by the Isle of Wight on that summer's afternoon was well-nigh indescribable. Rooty had worked things out pretty right, and there, among the glorious old trees, slightly on a rise, we could see Osborne House. Jove! it was good to be alive.

"What's the launch over there?" Dickie queried. The launch was the "Olympic," lying just opposite the hospital, having arrived with wounded the previous day.

We made straight for the wharf, and before we could say Jack Robinson, the old boat was moored bow and stern. There was no cheering crowd, only a few red-tabbed officials buzzing about, coming on board and going off again. Old Colonel Mac, the O.C., looked pretty worried, 'Auntie,' the Adjutant, was dashing about with bundles of papers, and big Fritz was following in his wake. Everything was excitement, although no one apparently had gone ashore yet. That was all we were concerned about, more specially when an hour passed and still everyone was on board.

"What the hell's wrong?' Smithy asked.

"Damned if I know," I replied.

"What about asking Fritz?" Jacko suggested.

I accordingly barged up to Fritz, "Say, when are they going to let us ashore?" I asked.

"Lucky if you get ashore at all," he shouted.

"How's that?" I wanted to know.

"Well, we've arrived unexpected as it were, they've never heard of us and don't bally well want to, and don't know what to do with us. Now you know as much as I do," and reeling this off, he stalked away.

Giving the boys this information, there was a riot of indignation, until better news arrived shortly after and we were lined up and told the position. We could go ashore until six o'clock, it was then 2.30, but we didn't argue about it. I've never seen a mob get ashore quicker. Most of the boys made for the nearest pub., they were anxious to try the English beer they'd heard so much about. We hadn't much cash, but everyone had enough for a spot.

Snowy and Lofty were first to line up at the bar and were still there at six o'clock. We guessed that's where we'd find them, so called on our way back and found Snowy explaining to the barmaid how many gallons of sea water he drank when the old boat was torpedoed.

Eventually we pushed Lofty and Snowy up the gangway and they were soon hauled aboard. The gangway was dropped, the bridge telegraph started the bells ringing, the engines were full astern, and we realised that our stay in England had certainly been short, if not sweet. Snowy said the scenery was great, but he must have meant the paintings on the walls of the Pier Tavern! At any rate, we chugged out the way we came and made straight for the other side.

At daylight next morning, we were lying off Le Havre, and by seven o'clock we were alongside. There seemed to be plenty of movement, boats going in and out, trains whistling their heads off, French and British troops everywhere, R.T.O.'s, Red Caps, M.L.O.'s, and the mob were on deck, eyeing everything. Apparently the most interesting thing was the mademoiselles; we were all anxious to 'parlez vous' with these damsels, they certainly looked 'tres bon.'

We were next dumped, bag and baggage, into the Rest Camp, some hole it was too, next door to the railway, and the rotten thing about it was, that once inside you couldn't get out without a pass.

It was after midnight during my first turn on guard, Dickie had just come off guard and I was taking his place, patrolling to and fro, when suddenly a searchlight flashed out and the sky was illuminated. Cocking my eye in its direction, I realised what was doing. Then there was a deafening explosion on the other side of the railway, quickly followed by another. There were now five searchlights scanning the sky, and I could hear the usual buzz of the engines: another explosion, a bit nearer this time. Those bally Huns were certainly familiar with our movements, seemed to be aware of our arrival and to arrange this as a sort of welcome.

A big fire, started by the first bomb, now helped to light up our surroundings, and we saw bombs dropping all over the show. There must have been half a dozen machines, the searchlights caught one, the guns opened fire, but he was gone again. After dropping about thirty more bombs, they vanished into the night and all was quiet again.

Thus passed our first night on French soil.

Once more we move, this time aboard the train, and we were pushed, ten or more into a small stuffy compartment. At eight p.m. the big, powerful French engine grunted and puffed out of the station, we knew not where to; all we'd been told was that the Somme was our destination.

After about thirty hours we steamed into Amiens. The station was one of those glass-roofed affairs, and an important junction, trains were coming and going the whole time, while troops lined the platforms. We were ordered to disembark, and were not sorry to stretch our legs. We then marched into a sort of square, where we partook of bully beef and biscuits, some of us hopping over and besieging the Y.M.C.A. Hut, the 'Joy Hut' they called it I believe, and joy it certainly was for us to get a wash and a cup of decent tea. After hanging around for some time, we were split up and billeted, some being sent to the old Saint Famille, and the rest of us to the

Lycee, right next to the station. It wasn't a bad show at all, and we soon set to and made ourselves as comfortable as we could.

For the first few days we were allowed a good deal of freedom and incidentally made a point of introducing ourselves to the mademoiselles. Saph and I set forth one evening with that express purpose and strolled down the main street first. Of course we had to make ourselves acquainted with Madame at the 'estaminet.' Old Madame Forgei Margueritte, she was a very oily old thing, fat and dirty.

"Oui, oui! soldat Nouvelle Zealande, tres bon abondance monnaie." Yes, she certainly had very nice girls.

"Oh well," said Saph, "give us some vin rouge instead." He didn't fancy the look of things, so we drank our first vin rouge and sauntered on a bit further. We walked some distance into the residential part of Amiens, among buildings, some demolished by shells, others, as we learned, by enemy bombs dropped from flying machines. Madame had told us that these machines came over at night, they would certainly come now that we were here, no doubt about that, they'd never failed yet.

Over to the right was the Cathedral, the stately edifice that had stopped a few shells in '14 and was now protected, high up, with sandbags. Inside we could see the Weeping Angel, the sacred child erected in memory of a famous priest of Amiens who had done so much for the little ones.

Amiens was all quiet, the silence being broken

only by the distant rumble of the guns. We walked smartly, for it was jolly cold and we weren't in a talkative mood. Just as we approached the station square quite late, I fancied I heard the purring of an engine. Saph heard it too. "Sounds like a machine," he said, and there was no doubt about it now, it was plainer than ever.

"One of ours returning," said Saph, and I thought it was too. We were now at the station and the machine was immediately overhead. A searchlight challenged it, nothing happened, it scanned the sky to and fro, and then another light flecked the darkness of the sky. That spinning noise started, faster and faster, nearer and nearer, it seemed almost to be coming down on our heads. We realised it was too dashed near and threw ourselves flat. As we touched the ground, the thing hit not a hundred yards away. There was a terrific explosion, followed immediately by another, this time hitting the station and hurling glass in all directions, the rails being bent and buckled and blown all over the show. In quick succession, more bombs followed, dropping around the station. Searchlights were busy, the anti-aircraft were blazing away, and we remained quite still for some considerable time until the fellow had apparently unloaded all he'd got.

Things were quiet for a bit and we decided to get, but after sprinting for a few yards, the noise started again, just behind us this time. Another machine arrived and its first bomb demolished a house opposite the station. We ducked once more,

trying to make ourselves as scarce as possible, and
I remember how the thought ran through my mind,
"Out of all this great big world, I've chosen you!"
I hoped this Hun wouldn't decide on me like the
bird once did. We sat tight until he'd dropped his
complement and then made another bid for it. We
got there this time, and damned glad we were too,
for the bombing continued until daylight.

Taking everything into consideration, we decided
we'd had a thrilling night's amusement. I don't
know what we looked like, but I know how we felt
at six-thirty parade that morning.

Orders were given that the G.O.C. of the
Division was visiting us at mid-day and a general
clean up was specified. The General arrived in
good time; we'd heard a lot about him, came out
to New Zealand as a gunner and worked his way
up. During the afternoon, I was detailed as orderly
corporal to conduct the inspecting party from one
camp to another. On nearing the second camp, the
General approached and said:

"Well, Corporal, how do the men like being in
France?"

"All right, Sir," I replied.

"Better than Egypt?" he inquired.

"Very much, Sir."

The thought then struck me that here was my
opportunity. I had been trying repeatedly to transfer to the Flying Corps and I felt that my O.C.
had blocked my application. Here then was the
very man to ask, seeing as how the G.O.C. Division
had to sanction the application. He seemed a

decent sort, so, risking the blast I expected to get
from my O.C., I said:

"I wish to transfer to the Flying Corps, Sir; is
there any chance?"

Funnily enough, he asked me the same question
as I'd had put to me by the Adjutant. "What, are
you tired of life?"

"No," I told him, "I just have a kink for it."

"Well," he said, "we don't wish to lose any of
our N.C.O.'s, but, if you're keen, there's a chance.
Two hundred vacancies to the Flying Corps have
just been allotted to the Anzac Division."

This was great news, and at this moment the
Adjutant butted in and I had to take a back seat.
I pictured a golden opportunity lost, but as the
General was leaving, he called me over.

"Still want that transfer, Corporal?" he asked.

"Too right, Sir," I replied.

"Well, renew your application in the morning."

I was too flabbergasted to thank him, but the
application went in, and within a week I was
ordered to appear before the Interviewing Officer
of the Flying Corps at Corbie. It certainly looked
as though my luck was in.

Major Boyd, the Interviewing Officer, was a
gruff Scotchman and an old pilot. I stalked into
the tent in my turn and he eyed me over critically.
I saluted as I'd never saluted before, for, as a rule,
we weren't too flash at that business, but I knew
what appearance meant. I'd got my chance and I
wasn't losing it.

He questioned me closely:

"Can you play football?"

"Can you ride?"

"Can you swim?"

"Can you row?"

"Have you ever been under shell fire?"

To all of which I said yes. He then questioned me about my weight. I was wearing a fur-lined British warm, which made me look heavier than I was. Apparently he doubted me and sent me with an orderly to the station to be weighed. On our return, he dismissed me, with no satisfaction, just said I'd hear one way or the other in due course. I didn't feel too happy after the interview, as I seemed to be possessed with the idea that he had taken a dislike to me. However, I had nothing to do but to wait and see.

On the way back to Amiens, an ambulance passed me and the driver offered me a lift, which was readily accepted. We took a rather round-about route and were passing the famous aerodrome at Bertangles when an officer hailed us. He was a flying chappie, decorated with wings and the M.C. He told us there had been a crash, the pilot was dead and he wanted us to take the body in to the hospital. How cheerful! and I'd just been doing my damnedest to get into this outfit. We pulled into the aerodrome and there, on the other side of the landing ground, lay all that was left of a perfectly good aeroplane. It had been on fire and was still smoking, and we saw that a gang of men were struggling with something. I hopped out of the ambulance to give a hand and found it was the dead pilot they were lifting. Poor devil, he was charred beyond recognition, and on looking closer, proved a truly terrible sight. This young dare-devil, who was no more, had, not two hours be-fore, left that very spot on a reconnaissance over the enemy lines, and in the pink of condition. Five Huns had pounced on him, he'd put up a great fight against tremendous odds. After shooting one of them down, he himself was hit, and with his machine riddled with bullets, managed to reach his aerodrome, only to crash. The engine caught fire and the flames did the rest. Some grit that kid had.

Several times during the next few days, my thoughts returned to this incident and I found myself debating the subject. "Don't be a fool," I thought, "get out of it while you can." Both the General and the Adjutant thought me an ass and had asked me if I was tired of life. They ought to know. Yes, this flying was a mug's game and damned dangerous too, I could see that. I'd back out of it, and yet, no, I couldn't do that, it was yellow, or looked like it. I'd certainly got the wind up a bit, but in any case, I thought, "one might as well be killed that way as any other." I reckoned that Fritz would get some of us with those bombs of his; he'd tried pretty hard and our luck couldn't always be in. Eventually I dismissed the subject and events took their course.

A fortnight after this incident, I received orders to report to the headquarters of the Flying Corps at St. Pol, away up by Abbeville.

The boys gave me a great send-off, and after a wonderful night of wine, women and song, I clambered into the train, feeling more dead than alive. Midnight the following night found me at St. Pol, still suffering from a head. I made for the nearest pub. in hopes of securing a few hours' sleep, but found a sing-song in process. It looked inviting anyway, so I barged in and saw six or seven of them around a very much out-of-tune piano, yelling the place down.

"Come on, Digger," one shouted, "join in." By the look of things, I concluded they must be celebrating something, so I asked the reason of all the jollification, and was told that they were all joining the Flying Corps and were really on their way to Blighty for training. This was great news to me, and they certainly looked a sporty crowd. I felt distinctly happy and introduced myself.

At the piano was a red-faced, chubby lad, a despatch rider, wearing the blue and white band round his arm. Chicko was his name, and I heard he got in the Schneider Cup Team, didn't agree with the chief, so got outed. Sitting on the piano was the proud possessor of a seven-a-side moustache, well waxed. This was Williams, known for his rendering of 'McNamara's Band,' not for flying: he crashed. Then there was big Brooky, six foot one, still with that creamy complexion of his baby days, to which no razor had as yet been applied. He was a despatch rider too; we went through together and back overseas. He made a landing in a Handley Page on the officers' mess

one night, and made a mess of himself. Spinky
was another, went through Oxford with him and
lost track of him afterwards. Little Wigley made
a great flyer, M.C.'s, D.F.C., bars, etc., to burn,
and broke up at last.

Apparently this happy party partook of the
lubricant often and much, and the early hours of
the morning found us, more or less sober, still
yelling. We were told eventually to stop that
bloody row and quit. Had it been anyone but a
red-tabbed Colonel, we should have told him to go
to hell, but as it was we went to bed ourselves.

Next morning found me with a head like a
bushel sieve. Brooky hauled me out with orders
to cut up to headquarters quick and lively, as the
train went at mid-day, and if I wanted to be with
the mob, I'd have to hop about. So, giving breakfast the go-by, I trooped up to the old Chateau,
where all the big bugs hung out, and was inter-
viewed by all and sundry, from the Sergeant to the
blinking Colonel. In the end I got what I wanted,
a ticket to Blighty, report to Farnborough, a spot
of leave, and then train for a pilot.

It was a happy crowd that landed at Victoria
Station the following afternoon. We made straight
for the old Strand Palace, spruced ourselves up
and set out to celebrate our first night in London.
What happened, or what we did, I've never been
able to find out. All I can remember is everybody
arm-in-arm, coming up the Strand, trying to sing
'Something Oriental' from 'Bing Boys,' and
then being piled into a taxi and Chicko insisting on

kissing the driver. The rest is a blank. One thing I do know and that is, my head was worse, if anything, when I wakened, than it was the morning before, and that neither Brooky nor I had to dress; we only had to get up.

Later that day, we went down to Farnborough; they gave us a fortnight's leave, so we said "Cheerio" to each other and went our own ways.

CHAPTER IV

PER ARDUA AD ASTRA

HAVE you ever spent a leave in England? Well, it's great, just to know that you are safe once again, if only for a while.

I made the Strand Palace my home. A Captain Johnnie, in the Guards, sat at the same table as myself and we got to talking about things in general. He wanted to know who I was and where I came from, and although I thought him pretty inquisitive, I had the common sense on that occasion not to say so. Anyway, the long and short of it was, that in the end he took me down to his parents' place for the week-end. He was on the staff in London.

Berkshire was the county, I remember that, and I also vividly remember the shock I received when we arrived at the little country station, and I saw a big Rolls Royce waiting. He directed me to it, and the biggest shock came when the chauffeur opened the door, ushered me into the back seat, and I saw the most delightful looking member of the opposite sex that it had been my luck to meet. I wanted to cuddle her right away, but I had to be formally introduced first. Yes, this was sister

Betty, and big brother Robert did the introducing.
I settled down beside her, with the determination
that this visit was going to be 'thumbs.'

The Rolls Royce glided along through delightful
country, an avenue of poplars appeared, and we
passed through them, finally arriving at a picturesque old building, which Betty told me was
home; not bad either, I thought.

Some joker in uniform met us at the door, and
was told to take me to the 'spare room.' I'd been
in spare rooms before and fell to wondering what
this one might be like. It proved to be no ordinary
room, in fact it was rather extraordinary. Everything was blue, except me, and I was feeling pretty
perky, for things promised to be interesting and
the girl, Betty, was a dream.

Downstairs, there were a lot more introductions
to be gone through. I hated it and felt a big ass,
like the Aussie when he called the fox by the
wrong name. Papa wasn't a bad old stick, but
Mamma eyed me up and down through her lorg-
nettes, very suspiciously, I thought. Auntie too
impressed me as a bit of a snag and seemed very
surprised because I was white.

"I thought all you New Zealand people were
black!" she said. Yes, she was a snag all right.

That night at dinner, I felt a bigger ass than
ever, with all the maids buzzing around waiting on
me, to say nothing of the array of knives, forks,
etc. I began to wish I was back with the boys,
where I could pick things up with my hands if I
wanted to. Robert was very decent, however, and

put me on the right track several times, and after a couple of days, I was quite at home. I appreciated these people's hospitality; they were real old English aristocrats, and I felt I had known them for years, instead of being almost a perfect stranger.

Betty, Robert and I enjoyed many a gallop. Gee! that girl could ride. Robert had to return to duty, while I was invited to stay if I wished. Of course I wished, wasn't the most beautiful maiden on earth there. At the end of a week, we were good pals, and then one night I made a mess of things. Yes, I went and proposed; it was really Papa's fault. It was my last night there, and he made the whiskies extra big, but Betty was a sport and forgave me in the morning.

So my first leave in England came to an end, and my next move was to report back at Farnborough.

It was winter 1916-17 and damned cold too. My newly-made friends at St. Pol turned up one by one.

We were bundled off to the Flying School at Denham, and for two months were put through physical jerks, slope arms, order arms, elementary topography, military law and so forth. The discipline at this place was strict, one Captain Robertson, a real Scot, who had stopped a Fritz's bullet at Mons, was our O.C. He delighted in rubbing in to us that we were going to be officers and must set an example. He had a dead set on anyone wanting leave and wasn't going to have his cadets running all over the country on railways, at the Army's expense. Ten per cent. only would be allowed out on leave during the week-ends, so the rest of us had to set to and devise some other means of getting away. It wasn't so bad getting out of camp as getting in again. Several of us joined the football team and that got us away for two or three week-ends. We went up to Oxford and over to Reading, playing there, and other week-ends we had to walk five miles up to Uxbridge before getting the Underground for the big city.

Returning on Monday morning was a harder proposition, however. We had to dodge any officers who were aboard the train and might ask to see our passes, so invariably waited until the train was almost on the move before dashing in.

Denham station only possessed one platform, so as soon as the train drew alongside, we hopped out on the other side, over the rails, and down the bank, where we waited until everyone was safely in camp and then made a dash for it. It nearly always came off all right, and when the six-thirty parade fell in and the roll call was taken, we were there.

It was a red-letter day for most of us when we passed out and moved on to the Advanced School at Oxford. Brooky and I shared a room in Queen's College, Chicko and Williams were on the same floor, and Len Issitt turned up too. He's the big bug now in New Zealand, Director of Aviation or something like that—Major, bless you! Below was Inky, Spinky, Watson, Happy Rud, Andy, and a real happy mob we were.

Here we were to learn engines, wireless, rigging theory of flight, machine guns, and a hundred and one other things. There wasn't any time for binges or merrymaking. It was just at the time when Fritz had the upper hand, casualties were heavy, and they were getting us through as quickly as possible, so it meant work, all work, morning, noon and night. Yes, even at night you darn well had to slog in at wireless. A constant buzz could be heard around the court, and there was sometimes so much row that you couldn't possibly read Morse.

Leave at Queen's College was an unheard-of thing. The only time we got out of the building was for our morning run and when marching round to the old museum where the lectures were given. And there was no means of getting out either; the walls around gave the place every appearance of a prison, while the guard at the gate was as conscientious as any warder. Nevertheless, we realised that we had a lot to learn and much swatting had to be done. We were all keen to get through and only hard work would do it.

So the weeks at Oxford passed very quickly, and then the exams. Gosh! how I had the wind up over them. I'd found it very hard getting down to arithmetic and study after years from school. I couldn't think quickly enough, but the Morse worried me most. As you may imagine, I had no desire to return to my unit, and that was what failure meant.

Four hundred of us sat down in the Oxford Town Hall for the final paper. Some bird rattled off Morse from the balcony and we had to take it down. Only two mistakes were allowed, and I was all right provided no one sneezed or made a noise. If that happened, I was done. Gee! I never opened my ears to that familiar dot, dash, as on that day, but there was no need for alarm, as it turned out, for all our crowd got through all right except poor old Rud. They kept him there another month and he passed eventually.

Before leaving Oxford, we were decked out in uniforms, equipment, Sam Brownes, not forgetting that 'Pip.' Actually a 'Pip' on each shoulder, and the weight was tremendous. Second Lieutenant, if you please, a blinking officer. Oh! yes, it was a great day, and of course we were all added to Papa Cox's list. A cheque-book was also a very essential part of our belongings.

The following day, seven of us rolled up at the orderly room of No. 4 Reserve Squadron, Northolt Aerodrome, and reported for flying. At Oxford, we had been asked if we wished to be posted to any special place, and Brooky and I both put in for Northolt, not far from the big city, as also did Watson, Chicko, Williams, Spinky, and Inky. That made the seven, and a bright mob we looked. Green wasn't the word for it, but we didn't stay green long.

Just a coincidence perhaps, yet strange, but the first aeroplane I saw was a Maurice Farman Shorthorn, and the first machine I flew in was of the same type, 'Rumpetys' they were called.

On a cold, misty morning, at the early hour of

six-thirty, the Instructor ordered me to climb into the front seat of 7066. I was about to be initiated into the mysteries of flying. These machines were queer-looking affairs, with the seat miles out in front of the plane, and it struck me that in the event of a sudden dive to earth on the part of the frail looking construction, the only thing between me and terra firma was a groggy looking piece of three-ply. I hoped 7066 would behave properly; what appeared to me to be the joystick, reminded me more of a pair of spectacles balanced on the top of an iron rod. I was told to grasp this, lightly at first, just to get the feel of things. I got my feet badly mixed up in the network of wires running along the floor of the seat; there seemed to be wires all over the thing. However, before I knew much about it, the old Raf engine was purring away behind us and we were sailing gaily over Harrow-on-the-Hill. It was too misty to see much and soon became so bad that we had to land, and my first flight ended without the least bit of excitement. The whole thing looked easy enough, but when I began to inspect the contraption we had been up in, I couldn't believe that it was possible to fly in the thing. It appeared more like a Chinese puzzle than anything else.

For the first week, my log-book read, one hour forty minutes dual.

"You're heavy on controls," Captain Archer said. He was the Instructor and not a bad sort.

"Got to get out of it, understand?" He impressed that upon me, but my only reply was a

grunt. Then he took me up for an hour to prac-
tise landing, but I only annoyed him by sticking
her nose down too much.

"Keep her nose up," he yelled, so I pulled the
stick back a bit and along we sailed, good-o as I
thought, when he suddenly bawled again, "Keep
her nose up." I pulled the stick back a good bit.
"Don't stall her," he shouted and pushed the stick
forward. Then I must have let her get her nose
down again, for he got very excited and pushed the
stick right forward, with the engine full on, until
the old rattle-trap, nose pointing to earth and me
in front, was doing about ninety. He bawled
again:

"That's right, go on, you bloody fool, now stick
her nose down and kill the two of us." So I reversed
her position and stuck her nose up once again.
Inky told me that from the ground it looked like a
steeplechase: at any rate, it cured me. The impres-
sion on my mind of that spot of earth I was going to
hit, was indelible; I'd no desire to make acquaintance
with that.

On my thirteenth day flying, I was told to go
solo. Thirteenth, gee! a good job I wasn't super-
stitious. It was a delightful day too, much too
good to crash. A sandbag was planted in my
previous front seat and I was promoted to the back
one, and away I taxied. It was a queer sensation,
going solo for the first time. However, I managed
to get her into the wind, pushed the throttle forward, and the old bus bounced away over the
ground. Back went the stick, gently does it, and

bless you, we were off the ground, up, up; goodness knows how many miles I went before I turned. I was too scared to look round. Then, a beautiful flat turn and the aerodrome seemed to be miles away. Round we went at a thousand feet; this was great, but I had been told not to go higher than five hundred feet and to do only one circuit of the aerodrome. The altimeter said two thousand, and I was still going round and round. It must have been nerves, for I was scared to shut the throttle off and come down. At last, however, I plucked up courage, and brought her round in order to come in for landing. Came in too high first time, gave it another go and went round once more, all right this time, only a bit short, so opened up the throttle, then a hedge loomed up suddenly and I realised that I'd overshot it, so throttled on again and did one more circuit. This time I gauged it O.K., the wheels touched, we bounced a few feet, the wheels touched again, a few more bounces, she ran a bit, then stopped. I'd done my first solo, and I taxied triumphantly to the hangars, conscious that my head was beginning to swell, until the Instructor said:

"Well, why the devil didn't you go round a few more times?" and then very sarcastically added:

"You'll run out of benzine one of these days."

I just smiled, a very sickly smile at that. At any rate, I'd taken an aeroplane up and got down without breaking my neck or smashing the machine, so he needn't be funny, I thought.

During the next two days, I did a bit over four hours solo. Brooky and all the mob were solo, and as the weather was fine, we got in all the flying we could. None of us liked the old Rumpetys, however, and were anxious to get on to something more exciting.

We finished flying at Northolt on a Friday, and it proved an unlucky day for some. There was an epidemic of crashes, no less than eleven, piled all over the ground. Everyone seemed to get the wind up after a Captain somebody crashed in an Avro and was killed. He certainly did it properly, a nose dive, and the thing was smashed to smithereens. After this everyone lost nerve, and a couple of Rumpetys decided to land at the same time, on the same spot, and made a nasty mess of it. The two pupils, who were solo, got badly smashed up. Another Rump overshot and landed in the hedge, throwing a pilot out like a horse throws its rider after a few somersaults in the saddle. He picked himself up, none the worse, but the old Rump had altered shape. For variety, another guy stood a Rump on her nose in the middle of the aerodrome, and this proved a magnet for somebody else, another soloist, who landed on top of it. So it went on all day, and Brooky and I decided it was time to get out of this show.

The next day our luck was in, and we were posted to No. 19 Squadron at Hounslow, together with Inky and Watson. This suited us, conveniently near the big city, not much of an aerodrome though, small, and you had to come in right over the town. There were plenty of wires to get tangled up in too, and at the top end was a brick affair, about thirty feet high, which looked like some old rifle butts, a rotten sort of thing to hit taking off.

There was one Squadron flying F.E.2.B.'s, while the Squadron we were posted to were flying D.H.I.'s, and not bad little buses either. Our instructors were one Lieut. Stewart, a ranker, good chap too, and a great bird at spinning. I think he was the first to spin one of these D'H.'s, and I wasn't satisfied until I got him to do it with me in the front seat; it was great.

Baldwin Raper was another instructor, who managed to find time, between buying timber and attending Parliament, to do some flying. I think every policeman in Hounslow knew him, or at least those who patrolled the main road to town. His slowest speed was fifty, and I heard he hit one or two things, but that's only by the way. He could certainly fly, and I see by my log-book that he gave me my first hour on D.H.'s. The second day he gave me twenty landings, one after the other; must have thought I would need 'em.

Major Morton was O.C., while Jacky Medford was Adjutant. I won't say anything about him, except that his Pa used to write sometimes about croquet, and Jack, well, he stood on the mess table once and recited. It was summer and he hadn't much on either.

Well, here we started to fly in earnest, and were keen about it too. We had plenty of lectures and machine gun practice. Brooky and I did some photography together from the air, but could seldom find the pin point. I remember how, one day, intent on doing the job properly, we nearly got tangled up with one of those observation balloons at Barnes. Then we had a bit of formation practice, which I used to enjoy thoroughly.

One glorious morning, Lieut. Stewart said he'd take some of us down to Shoreham. He led the way, Brooky was on his right, I was on the left, while behind us came Watson and a chappie named Ball. Soon after starting, Brooky and Watson dropped out with dud engines, so the three of us had to go on without them. It was delightful going until nearing the coast, when we ran into a thick fog. Stewart knew where the aerodrome was, we didn't. However, I saw he had throttled back and was diving down through the mist, so I followed, with Ball behind me. I was soon in a hopeless maze and couldn't see a couple of yards. It was my first experience of the kind and I didn't know whether I was upside down or what; I did know that I had no desire to hit the ground, so I pulled the old bus up, put the throttle full over, and flew straight on, travelling for some distance, still in a thick mist. I hadn't the least idea where I was, or in what direction I was flying.

Suddenly the mist disappeared and I found myself flying over the sea, with nothing but water in every direction.

"Hell!" I thought, "where am I now?"

Landing on the briny ocean was no good to me,

so I turned her round and flew back into the fog, and after a few minutes decided to come down a bit. I accordingly throttled back and stuck her nose down, and found the mist had cleared somewhat. Then a bridge loomed up and I was apparently flying straight for it, on went the engine again, back went the stick, and up into the mist once more. I must have flown round and round, for the next time I stuck her nose down, a row of bathing sheds seemed to be coming at me, and I couldn't have been twenty feet above the beach. I zoomed over them and into the mist, trying once more to locate this infernal aerodrome. I remembered that an instructor had once told me I'd run out of benzine some day; perhaps this was going to be the day; goodness knows how long I'd been cruising round, and there were no compasses or instruments much on this old bus, or I might have done better. However, I gave it another go, and through the mist spotted what appeared to be a big, open space, where I eventually decided to land. The wheels touched—it was a ploughed field—we ran a few yards and ended in a most graceful somersault, the machine lying there on her back, with me underneath. Oil, or something sticky, started trickling on my face, stacks of it, until eventually I managed to crawl from underneath, just as some women, who were hoeing in a nearby field, came running up. They seemed very disappointed, for one exclaimed:

"Oh! he's not killed," and the tone of her voice prompted me to say:

"No, I'm sorry to disappoint you; would you like me to do it again?"

With the Hun crash helmet I was wearing pushed down, nearly hiding my face, which was covered with oil, and my clothes a combination of oil, water and dirt, I must have looked a dream. And the annoying part of it all was that the aerodrome was not a quarter of a mile away. I 'phoned up from a nearby farmhouse and found that Stewart had landed all right, but they hadn't heard anything of Ball, although by the time a tender arrived for me, we learned that Ball had crashed. He arrived without notice in someone's back yard and hit a house-top in process. Both he and the machine were done for—no more flying.

A little later, the mist had cleared, and after arranging about the crashed machine, Stewart said he'd take me back to Hounslow. The chaps at Shoreham hadn't seen a D.H. spun, so, with me in the front seat, and just that piece of three-ply between me and the ground, he spun that old bus again and again, telling me afterwards that it was for my especial benefit. I told him he needn't have troubled, but any way he said the formation was a wash-out, and seeing that only one machine out of five took the return trip, I agreed with him.

A few days after this, I took a new bus on a cross-country flight. It was a delightful spring day, and I flew along at three thousand, past the Welsh Harp and Hendon aerodrome to London Colney, where I had lunch and made a few new acquaintances. Just as I was about to leave, my

Squadron rang up with orders for me to remain there until further notice, as a Gotha raid was in process over London. It sounded exciting, and everyone was keyed up to concert pitch. Twenty-two of the blighters came over, in perfect formation, dropping their pills everywhere. We all felt we'd like to stick a machine gun in any old bus and go up to have a pop at them. One guy from Northolt risked it on one of the first Bristols; he was an old overseas pilot. An observer volunteered, they got over the Huns, dived down through the formation and broke it up. But the observer, poor devil, was shot through the neck, and died before the machine landed. It was dashed impudent of those Huns in broad daylight, but London had no aerial defence in those days, a thing I could never understand.

Some time after tea, I got word that everything was O.K. and I flew back, arriving at dusk without further excitement. The O.C. at London Colney was a decent chap, some crack pilot, but the day after my visit there, the wing came off a Spad at four thousand and it dropped like a stone; he went west.

After an altitude test, Brooky, Inky, Watson and I were transferred to F.E.2.B.'s. These old buses always reminded me of playful elephants, pushers with one hundred and sixty Beardmore engine. We soon got going in them and did solo in a couple of days, to say nothing of wireless and having great fun with the aerial.

This sixty feet of copper wire, with its lead

weight attached, had to be let out after you got up and wound in again before landing. The two items to remember, and most of us forgot, were, not to let it out too fast, or it would break the lead weight off, and when the wire was all out, not to forget to wind in again before landing. That was all very well; my memory was good too, even if a bit short, and on the second morning I landed, trailing sixty feet of copper wire behind me, and numerous other articles collected by it in the process. I didn't get such a blast as Watson did the following morning, however, for he let his aerial out with a bang, the weight parted company with the wire, ending up on a breakfast table, where an aged couple were eating. The poor old lady nearly died of shock, and so did 'Waty' when he found the weight gone from his aerial.

My old pal, Rooty, turned up at the aerodrome one day and requested a flip. He was game all right, for I hadn't done twenty hours solo then. The instructor said he'd shut his eyes, however, and away we went.

I showed him Richmond and Kew from the air and Rooty took a few photos, until in his excitement he dropped his camera overboard. He yelled out to me:

"What about stopping, I've dropped it."

But just then something else happened, the engine cut out, so I yelled back to him:

"The damned engine heard you, it's stopped."

I tried a few of the gadgets, but nothing happened, so the only alternative was to look out for

5

a forced landing, which eventually took place in a wheat field, nose up. Rooty was shot out, followed by the benzine tin, which served him for a seat, and which cracked him on the head, while I had incidentally knocked the under-carriage off.

"Do you always land like this?" was Rooty's first remark, to which I replied:

"Occasionally, but at any rate, you said you wanted to stop, so you can look for your camera."

I 'phoned the aerodrome, and was told to stand by, while a curious crowd seemed to come from nowhere. I decided that my passenger had better disappear, in case of a strafe; I'd just about get court-martialled for having a passenger aboard.

To Rooty's disgust, I told him he'd have to walk, but his reply doesn't bear repeating. At any rate, I reported that I'd gone up solo and had forgotten the ballast for the front seat. Someone called me a damn fool and that was that. Rooty had his flip and I had crash number two; bad habit this crashing.

Each of us had had about ten hours solo on F.E.'s when our instructor told us we'd have to do a few night landings, and providing we didn't smash anything, we might be presented with a pair of wings. We weren't too keen on this night flying, groping around in the dark trying to find the ground at its right level. No! it didn't appeal to any of us, daylight suited us better, you could see what you were doing. The wings were a great inducement, however, and the quartette, Inky, Watson, Brooky and I, were all to have a shot.

And very relieved we were too when it was over. No one crashed, more by good luck than skill, although poor old Watson got the wind up. The infernal searchlights went out just as he was coming in to land, so he tootled round and round until they got them going, some twenty minutes later.

The next day we were informed that we were now full-blown pilots, and of course we all had wings ready to pin on. Our heads swelled almost to pumpkins before next morning, and Brooky had to get a new hat.

We celebrated the auspicious occasion by a night in town. Brooky wanted to see 'Baby Mine,' so we all rolled along to the theatre, discovering later that Brooky's keenness was due to the fact that Iris Hoey was in the lead and wore a very dainty pink nightie most of the time. Pink was Brooky's favourite colour. We lost him after the show, so we hired a taxi and saw London by night. Goodness knows where we went. Inky declared we were all sober, although I had my doubts. I remember Inky insisted on posing as Cupid in Piccadilly, and the rest of us having to talk politely to a burly policeman, who wanted to run him round to Vine Street. We talked him round eventually, but Inky started again. He remembered, he said, that it should be done in the nude, complete with bow and arrow, and started to disrobe. In the end we had to bundle him into another taxi and drive round once more, finishing up at the 'Cri.' Next morning, we found ourselves in bed at the Regent Palace.

At mid-day, back at the aerodrome, Inky decided to take the air, to blow the cobwebs off. The engine in 1654 had a nasty habit of cutting out, and it did the same thing on this particular occasion, landing Inky on someone's back lawn. It turned out to be a pastor's place, quiet and romantic, and there was a daughter. At any rate, Inky often used to disappear in that direction and circle round over a certain place.

We wondered what was to become of us now that we were qualified. Casualties were very heavy in the Flying Corps about this time and we expected to be dumped straight away overseas. Whilst keen about this, we felt that a bit more experience would be helpful, for after all, we'd only done about thirty hours solo, not much to go scrapping on, especially in F.E.'s, against Huns on Fokkers.

A few days later, however, we were sent for and instructed to proceed to the aerial fighting and gunnery school at Turnberry, in Scotland. We'd heard good reports of this place and were tickled to death. It certainly came up to expectations. The Great Western Hotel was our billet, a bedroom overlooking the sea, dainty maids trotting here and there, golf links, etc. We began to wonder where the War was, and if there was one at all.

They made you work though, parade at six-thirty, and machine guns till dark. Targets of all descriptions, gadgets everywhere, things popping up all over the show. The aerial cage was a great stunt, a machine gun mounted on the cage, you climbed in and away you went. A machine flew out at sea, and whilst the cage travelled through the air, you had to pot at the machine's shadow on the water. Of course it was arranged that the gun jammed half-way across and you had to put it right; that was one of the tests. Clay pigeons were popular and I often won enough bobs at this sport to shout drinks. The best fun, however, was chasing a Hun machine, one that had been brought down, in a B.E., Vickers or an F.E., and potting at him with a camera gun, then waiting to see the result, when the film would tell you whether you had registered a hit or not. It was great fun, and we couldn't get enough of this, but a storm blew everything down one night, smashed several of the machines and was the cause of our stay in this delightful spot being somewhat shortened. The place was badly situated for an aerodrome. We packed our bags and proceeded to York.

Here we were informed that we four had been chosen to concentrate on night flying. I say we four, but we seemed to hang together, and we were very disappointed over this night flying, not a bit keen. Night flying was in its infancy then, and it seemed to us that there was more fun and excitement flying by day, although later we found out that we were wrong in this.

York sent us on to 33 Squadron, just outside Lincoln, where we were informed, on arrival, just to cheer us up, that the Adjutant was away at a funeral.

There had been an accident while night flying, the pilot and observer both being killed, due to the machine catching fire. The orderly room clerk was very decent, gave us all the details, how the machine crashed, burst into flames, and how the poor fellows shouted and screamed before they were burnt to death. So thoughtful of him to tell us just what happened. At any rate, we knew what to expect, and he looked rather sorry for us when we told him that we were reporting for night flying.

"Dangerous game, Sir, we've had quite a number of accidents here," he said. At this juncture, however, we withdrew, we'd had enough for a start.

Our stay here was to be of longer duration than we at first thought, and after a few hours at this dangerous game, as the clerk called it, which we survived without loss of life, Brooky, Waty and I were posted as Home Defence Operation Pilots, much to our disgust. We were anxious to get overseas now, for with our additional experience we felt confident to put up a good show. Inky was the only lucky one and he got on to day flying. He got through all right too; read of his wedding awhile back, flash affair in London.

This Home Defence job was no good, it meant doing patrols and hunting the sky for Zepps. We were flying antiquated machines half the time, couldn't get any height, and the rottenest part was that we couldn't get any promotion until we had been overseas.

Nevertheless, the extra experience gained in those few months of Zepp strafing stood us in good stead when we did eventually get overseas.

CHAPTER V

NIGHT FLYING

OUR new aerodrome was a good one and a decided change after Hounslow. It was about three-quarters of a mile long, with a good width. In addition to the Home Defence Flight, there were two training squadrons flying Avros, B.E.'s and an odd Spad or two. There was plenty of activity.

Our machines were F.E.2.B.'s, equipped with one hundred and sixty Beardmore engine. A machine gun was fixed to the front seat, to be used by the observer. There were three machines, with the same number of pilots and observers for operation. Emergency landing flares, which could be ignited by pressing a button in the cockpit, were fixed under each of the lower planes. A parachute flare could also be dropped from the back seat. This would hang in the air and light up the ground for about three minutes. There were also three other machines, used for training purposes.

Ours was A Flight, while B and C were thirty miles north and west. Our patrol was north to the Humber and ten miles south of Lincoln.

After a few flights, we realised that these buses were totally unfit for the job. They were not capable of climbing higher than about twelve thousand feet, while the Zepps seldom came over at less than eighteen to twenty thousand. We expressed our views and were granted permission to do anything with the machines to enable them to get higher. This caused tremendous competition between the three of us. Ceiling tests were frequent, without producing anything startling until the engine was taken out of my bus and a three hundred Rolls Royce put in. With this extra power, we expected something great, but even then, old 1884 would not go higher than sixteen thousand, and it took nearly an hour to get there. I did away with the observer, put the machine gun on to a mounting to enable the pilot to use it, placed a cowling over the front seat and streamlined it, and then re-rigged her. But I only got another hundred feet, so we took the cowling off again. It seemed pretty hopeless trying to get Zepps in these antiquated machines.

England's aerial defence at this time was pretty rotten, and the Hun could have done what he liked with us had he known. That's what makes me think that his secret service couldn't have been what it was cracked up to be, or he would have known just how weak our defence was. However, we did our best in the circumstances. I think Robinson, Brandon, Tempest and those chaps must have got their Zepps at lower altitudes, probably when they came down to do their bombing. They were in B.E.'s and perhaps got a bit more out of them than we did out of our old Fees.

The Huns' Zepp Base was at Heligoland, due east of Spurn Head. His course was due west until he struck Spurn Head, where he would pick up the lights of Hull, invariably turning south and passing right over our aerodrome, then picking up Lincoln and apparently following the Northern Railway down to London. He always came in what we called the dark period, when there was no moon, and during this time we were not allowed to leave the aerodrome after dark, operation pilots standing by the whole time, with machines ready and ears pricked up every time the telephone bell rang. We always hoped it would be orders to take the air, our first intimation usually being from the Navy. "Zepps sighted forty miles east Spurn Head, proceeding west," later, "Zepps still proceeding west, now twenty miles from coast." At this stage, the first operation pilot would be ordered up with certain instructions, the remaining two at ten-minute intervals. Our patrol was for three hours, and we took our turn in being first.

Owing chiefly to the fog, England was not the best of countries for flying, particularly at night. The fog was our worst foe, and being near the coast, we had to be extra careful not to go wandering out over the sea, a matter very easily accomplished at night in a fog. Two or three of our chaps went west that way, and we never heard of them again. We could only conclude that the North Sea claimed them as victims.

On the twenty-first of August, 1917, I took the air in quest of Zepps for the first time. We received our first news of them at ten-thirty p.m., and at eleven o'clock, Robiers and I taxied out, having been given a great send-off. All the pupils from the training squadrons used to turn out to see our show and would hang about all night for our return.

We circled the aerodrome for some time to gain height and then turned north, registering five thousand. The night was beautifully clear and starlit, but cold, and we tootled along past the blast furnaces at Scunthorpe, where the reflection could be seen for miles. No doubt the Hun knew the position of this furnace and it would help him to get his bearings. Why they didn't try to lessen the flare we could never understand, and it was some considerable time before they thought to do so.

By the time we reached the Humber, our height was ten thousand, and again we circled round and round to get higher, both piercing the darkness with bulging eyes in the endeavour to glimpse a target. Seeing a searchlight pop up over Hull, we set our nose in that direction, and soon there were about half a dozen, lighting up the sky. This show promised well. We were now over the Humber, just about where the ZR2 broke her back some time later. We were hoping to break the back of a Zepp before long.

I don't know what Robie's eyes were like, but mine seemed to be nearly out of my head by this time. Shells were bursting all over the place, although there was no sign of the Zepp as far as

I could see. Our altimeter showed twelve thousand. Gee! this old bus was slow, but I had a feeling that our luck was going to be in. We were now off our patrol, but what did that matter so long as there was something doing. The gun-fire stopped and the searchlights were scanning to and fro, an almost certain sign that they'd lost him. Our hopes went down correspondingly, as one by one the searchlights lowered, until all was darkness again, and the Zepp went gaily on her errand of destruction.

We groped around for another two hours, realising that we'd been pretty near, and still not wishing to give up all hope, saw the remaining hour out and then, benzine being low, were obliged to land. We longed for the next raid and began to feel that after all there was a certain amount of fun in Zepp hunting, never knowing when you might spot one, even if he was five thousand feet above you.

Brooky and Watson were both down when we arrived. Like us, they had seen the gun-fire and sat with bulging eyes. No one got a Zepp that night, but poor old Joe, one of B Flight's pilots, crashed on landing and was killed.

The next dark period was a disappointing one; the Huns left us alone and we were very peeved. All kinds of new gadgets had been invented and adorned the cockpits. Reid, my new observer, was itching to hunt the skies, and we did a good deal of night flying without incident or crashes, save for one fatality, for which I was responsible.

We were carrying out forced landings one night and I pushed the parachute flare through the tube, but it failed to ignite. A few days later, a bill for twenty-five pounds was presented to me by a farmer, who called at the aerodrome with the complaint that the flare had hit his pet horse on the head. The following morning, Tony did not answer the roll call.

About this time, the Americans sent over two hundred of their picked men for the Flying Corps. The heads didn't know what to do with them, as the training squadrons were all going hard with our own pupils. Eventually they sent a few to each Home Defence Flight and in our spare time we were told we could teach them something.

Eight of them turned up at our Flight, good chaps too, and we enjoyed their company. Big Jeff was full of good humour, stood six feet odd and weighed about fifteen stone. I pictured him trying to get into the cockpit of a Spad or Sopwith Pup, but anyway, our Jeff turned out a good flyer and flew in the Dole Race.

Ned was a great boy, too, full of Yankee stories, and he used to have competitions with Sid to see who could yarn the most. They introduced all sorts of new drinks into the mess, port flips, egg flips, all sorts of flips. One of their number would get up and act as shaker, mixing the concoction, then shaking at considerable length in a metal tumbler arrangement with a lid. After it was shaken into what appeared to be all froth, he would triumphantly hand you the mixture, and if you blew the froth off, you blew the drink away. Nevertheless, the port flip was quite a decent thirst quencher.

These chaps were the keenest mob for flying I ever struck. They were willing to go up any time, in any weather, and with anyone, irrespective of their ability as a pilot. Jeff loved speed and I used to take him up in the F.E.2.D. which I used for operations. The machine did about ninety full out, which in those days wasn't bad.

On one occasion we were up about five hundred feet, when he yelled over from the front seat.

"Won't she go any faster?"

"Yes," I called back, "you watch her." I accordingly stuck her nose down, with the engine full on, and lowered to about fifty feet off the ground and one hundred and forty miles per hour holding her there until I thought the wings might buckle, and watching Jeff all the time. He never grabbed hold of the sides until he thought I'd gone mad and was going to fly straight into the earth, then I pulled her up in a great zoom, finishing up in a climbing turn. He turned round as I flattened out again and at first his face was a blank, then it suddenly lit up and he yelled:

"Gee! boy, that was great." He'd had his first real thrill in the air, he said. The next time I took him up, we reached twelve thousand and his nose started to bleed all over the show. He was in some pickle by the time we got down and I told him it was due to too many port flips. Jeff was annoyed and asked me not to let any of the boys know. He was afraid it might be looked upon as a physical defect and be the result of his getting chucked out. I believe that would have sent him potty, he was so keen.

We did lots of bombing practice and machine gunning for these chaps, and now and then a little visiting to the other Flights. C Flight over at Kelstern was a favourite flip for Jeff and myself.

Our next Zepp raid did not take place until October eighteen. Something must have gone wrong that night. We had a warning and were up at the Hangars, machines ready and flares alight, with the usual crowd to see the fun. We were standing by our machines and I was booked to take the air first, when, without any warning, there was a terrific explosion on the far side of the landing ground, followed by another at not half a minute's interval.

Even then we did not realise what it was until Reid, my observer, who was standing by, grabbed my arm and said:

"Listen, can't you hear it?" There was no doubt about it now, a Zepp was right overhead and there were we, still on the ground, waiting for orders to go up. The Zepp had seen our landing lights. We waited no longer for orders, Reid swung the prop, kicked the chocks away, hopped in and off we went, realising that it was a golden opportunity lost. A Zepp and right over our aerodrome; how on earth it had got so far without our receiving orders, puzzled us. Someone had been lax of course, and by the time we reached any height worth mentioning, the Zepp was probably fifty to a hundred miles away.

We patrolled to and from the Humber to south of Lincoln, and two hours passed. Having nothing to do, we were frozen, and I gazed overboard, to see the landing lights of an aerodrome burning. We turned north again, noticing the beauty of the starlit night, although, as we neared the river once more, things appeared rather hazy, and by the time we had reached our most northerly point and turned south, nothing could be seen at all. The familiar ground lights had disappeared and we seemed to have run into a cloud, so we continued south for a bit, thinking we were somewhere near our own aerodrome. We came lower to see what it was like—at fourteen thousand everything was thick, fog everywhere. Pulling the throttle back, we dived down a couple of thousand feet, but it was still so thick that I couldn't see Reid's head in the front seat. I was obliged to fly by the bubble to keep her on an even keel and came down to three thousand. Trying a few miles in every direction in hopes of finding a clear patch, proved without avail, dense fog enveloped everything. We couldn't even find our way down at a few hundred feet, our three hours was up and I knew that our benzine supply must be pretty low. Anyhow, we had to land somewhere, but where? We were in a rotten hole. Reid called over:

"What are you going to do?"

"Land as soon as I can see where to," I replied,

then turned her north and decided to give it another ten minutes. My altitude was showing three hundred feet. Fortunately it was flat country and I knew we were pretty safe, my only fear being that we might get out to sea, as the coast was only twenty miles from our aerodrome, and in such a dense fog it was easily done.

After proceeding north for a short time, Reid yelled excitedly:

"Lights, slightly to the port side."

We made for them right away, came down to one hundred feet and flew round a few times.

"What do you make of them?" I yelled to Reid.

"Looks like an emergency landing," he said.

It certainly did too, for there was the long and short arm of the letter L dimly discernible through the fog. The parachute flare lit all right when I pushed it through, but it seemed to make matters worse and increase the haze near the ground. Waiting for it to burn out, I decided I'd have to land without lights. We couldn't have been fifty feet up now and I turned round into position, and throttling back in the fog, misjudged the distance. Before either of us knew anything, we had hit the ground. Reid was thrown clear, turning a complete somersault as he left the bus, while I managed to knock out some teeth on the dashboard. The machine presented a good picture, with crushed under-carriage and tail up in the air.

Two mechanics who were posted at these emergency stations came rushing out.

"All right, Sir?" one inquired.

"Yes, and damned glad to get down," said Reid. "Give us a cigarette."

"Gosh, you weren't half lucky, Sir," the mechanic said, "we heard you for some time up in that fog, wonder you didn't knock the top off something flying around here."

Next morning, we realised just how true his words were. We had landed at an emergency ground just south of the Humber, and our O.C. had rung up, hoping to get news of us. They had tried to recall us with rockets owing to the bad weather coming.

With the aid of these rockets, Brooky and Watson got down all right and we wished we had done the same. Still, we were safe, although I felt annoyed that the old bus was damaged.

We arrived back at our aerodrome the following afternoon, and found them relieved beyond measure to know of our safety. One of C Flight's had forced landed the same as ourselves, and one of B Flight's had not been heard of. The worst was feared, and our suspicions were verified a few days later when some wreckage of a plane was found by a trawler in the North Sea.

This Zepp strafing job wasn't much good, so Brooky and I decided to put in a request to be transferred overseas.

That night, the Zepps had a bad spin too, five being brought down one way and another. One surprised a sector in the southern part of the line in France, by looming out of the fog just over their heads in the early hours of the morning, giving them good target practice.

A week after this incident, Brooky and I were sent down to Lympne, near Folkestone, to ferry two new buses back to Scampton. We left Lympne about three o'clock in the afternoon of a winter's day and reckoned on reaching Hounslow in order to spend the night there. On arriving at dusk, the O.C. seemed like a bear with a sore head, must have had a night out, we thought. At any rate, he told us we couldn't stay there, his hangars were full up.

"And you can't leave new machines out all night," he said, "you'll have to go on to Hendon." There was a bit of mist about too, and we knew we had valuable planes with us. It had been impressed on us before leaving that we could not, on any account, take risks with them. We were keen to land the machines safely at Scampton, so there was nothing for it but to push on, more especially as the O.C. ordered us to leave. We arranged to keep together, both knowing the country pretty well, and providing we could pick up the Welsh Harp, we would be all right. It was quite near Hendon aerodrome, but the landing ground in those days was not good, just a three-cornered place, with the railway running along one side.

Immediately we got up, we lost sight of one another, and the increasing darkness gave us no time to look round. Luckier than Brooky, I eventually picked up the Welsh Harp, and was set. Landing in the dark, however, I very narrowly escaped disaster, for my wheels touched ground not two yards away from a large hole in the middle of the aerodrome, made by the Huns in their last raid. I could just see a flag sticking up as I passed over, and wondered why the dickens it hadn't been filled in before. I went and had a look at it, and realised how near a smash I'd been.

Brooky and I had previously arranged, in the event of being parted, to meet at the Strand Palace, and I waited about for him, but he failed to put in an appearance until just after nine o'clock. He had landed down at Northolt and was obliged to wait for a train to town.

The following three or four days proved impossible for flying, thick fog predominating everywhere. We went to our respective aerodromes each morning, hanging around all day for nearly a week, until one morning I rang our O.C. at Scampton, to learn that the weather was all right there and received orders to try and get through. By ringing aerodromes on the way north, we found that the fog was only in a fifteen mile radius, so I decided to give it a go and rang Brooky at Northolt to that effect. He was agreeable, so I left Hendon and stuck to the Great Northern Railway track, flying no higher than one hundred feet, until, a little north of Hatfield, the fog disappeared and we ran into perfect weather conditions. We eventually landed at Scampton just after lunch, with everything O.K. The new buses were the centre of great attraction, being absolutely the latest, and we handed them over with feelings of relief.

Less than eight hours after our return, we were in the air again looking for Zepps. Our disappointment was great when we discovered that the new machines were not equipped for operations, for we had hoped to have accomplished something with them. Our chances with the old machines were pretty remote and nothing happened worth recording.

There was one more fatality, Solomon, a New Zealander, went west.

Christmas was approaching and the days were spent mostly in flying our American pupils, practising bomb dropping and machine gunnery. At night it was the same thing, with a bit of searchlight dodging thrown in. There was another casualty too, Livingstone, another New Zealander, sideslipped coming in and crashed, the machine catching fire. Livingstone was a live wire, great on the ivories, and we missed him very much.

C Flight had a nasty accident the same night, a machine landing at one of the emergency grounds, and when taking off, flew straight into a farmhouse, knocking half of it down and giving the poor old farmer and his wife, who were in bed, a rude awakening, in addition to having to dig their way out of the debris in the dark. Fortunately, nothing caught fire, although the pilot was injured beyond recognition.

There was an occasional raid, but our luck was out and we got disheartened, more and more anxious to be off overseas. Christmas passed and still nothing exciting beyond the fact that everyone

was blotto and suffered with heads for days afterwards. Boxing night, things were pretty willing,
Brooky and Pad announcing just after midnight
that they wanted to fly. We all went up to the
hangars and got the machines out into the moonlit
night without needing the flares. Why someone
didn't break his neck is hard to say, for we did
all sorts of mad things, and in the end lost Brooky
and Pad. We thought they must have forced
landed somewhere and carried on until four in the
morning. They hadn't turned up then, so we returned to the mess and saw the break of day whilst
sipping cocktails.

About eleven o'clock in the morning, when we
were all peacefully sleeping, the telephone bell went
mad. Brooky and Pad had just awakened and
found themselves at Retford aerodrome, where
they had gone to see the boys and have a spot.
They had been put to bed and knew no more until
the morning saw them in fresh surroundings, and
they thought they'd better let us know. The O.C.
was away when they left, but had a few words to
say on their return, and told Brooky, when he did
turn up, that the sooner he went overseas the
better, to which Brooky heartily agreed.

The funny part of it was that the following
morning, orders came through for Brooky and I
to report at Adastral House at once. Just what
we wanted, and we couldn't pack quickly enough,
for we knew it meant overseas for us. This loafing
on Home Defence was no good at all; all very well
for chaps who had been flying overseas, but not for

us. A tender was ordered, and with several rounds of drinks, we said "Cheerio" to 33 Squadron.

At Adastral House, we were given our tickets and told to embark on the seven o'clock train from Victoria the following morning.

We set to and enjoyed our last night in dear old London, and it was some night too. I went over to Portland Place, and rounded up some of my nurse friends, Brooky dropped into Selfridge's and picked up a couple of his pals, and we all met back at the Strand Palace, where we fell in with three more chaps we'd been through Oxford with. They were also for overseas duty, so we persuaded them to join our party and bring their lady friends. In the end, we mustered fourteen all told.

A table was set for us in the grill room, and after a couple of rounds of appetisers, we adjourned for the feed. At dinner, someone discovered that it was Jerry's birthday, so he was obliged to shout some fizz and we promoted him to the top of the table, calling for a speech. On rising to oblige us, he knocked his drink over, and as the bottle was empty, shouted another, and this time he drank it before he rose.

He started off, "On behalf of the widows and orphans," and suddenly got an inspiration, changing the subject to the declining birth rate. Then he got hiccoughs badly, sat down, and everyone agreed that it was the right way to finish up a birthday speech.

Three hours later, we were on the platform at Victoria, no farewells to make, we'd had them all the night before. We staggered into seats aboard the train, made ourselves as comfortable as possible, and as the train pulled out on its way to Folkestone, tried to secure some of the sleep we'd lost the night before.

No one spoke, but we all wondered when, if ever, we'd see dear old London again.

EACH EVENING AT DUSK THE USUAL PROCEDURE WAS GONE THROUGH

THERE MUST HAVE BEEN ALMOST A DOZEN SEARCHLIGHTS AFTER US

I TOOK THE AIR IN QUEST OF ZEPPS FOR THE FIRST TIME

WE TURNED AND THROTTLED BACK ONCE MORE TAKING
ANOTHER DIVE AT HIM

I COUNTED FIVE OTHER MACHINES FLITTING ROUND HAVING A LOOK

MY FAITHFUL OLD 2C ROARING DOWN THE FLARE PATH AND TAKING OFF IN GOOD STYLE

I TRIED A DODGE, AND LET GO THE PARACHUTE FLARE

"HE'S GOT HIM", SOMEONE YELLED

APPARENTLY HE DID NOT SEE US, FOR HE FLASHED PAST

LT. KINGSFORD IN HIS FE2B PRIOR TO FLIGHT TEST.
Note black and white dolls insignia painted on cockpit side; these two
miniature woollen dolls were given to him by a little French schoolgirl
and were hung on the dashboard during raids as a lucky emblem.

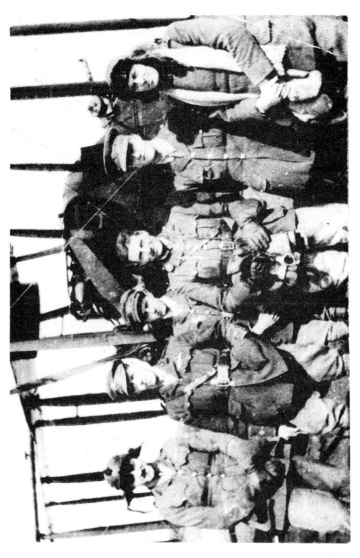

A.R. KINGSFORD IN 100 SQUADRON
(Left to Right: Lt. Bill Crofts (Pilot...P.O.W.), Lt. Linton-? (Pilot),
Lt. Sawyer (Observer..injured in crash), Lt. Bourne (Observer),
Lt. Siddaway (Pilot), Lt. Kingsford (Pilot)

FLYING LICENCE No.5013, 22 JUNE 1917

LOG BOOK

2ND LT. A.R. KINGSFORD WITH No.33 HOME DEFENCE SQDN.
(SCAMPTON) WHILST FLYING ANTI-ZEPPELIN PATROLS

CHAPTER VI

100 SQUADRON

IT was a miserable looking crowd which crossed the Channel on that particular day. Most of them had been home on a spot of leave and knew only too well to what they were returning. Like us, no doubt many of them had spent their last night in Blighty in a happy mood, and were feeling the effects. To make matters worse, it was choppy, and many were already 'hors de combat' laying about all over the deck. Rifles and equipment were scattered here and there, and some of the fellows were using their packs for pillows. Why these poor devils had to carry rifle and equipment with them on leave, and lug it perhaps up to the north of England, or some place equally far, always got me beat. Just as though it couldn't have been dumped at Boulogne and left for ten days. To forget it for a bit would have been good I know.

Our escort was busy on the look-out for prowling under-sea enemy craft. These dapper little destroyers fascinated me, darting here and there, in every direction. On such craft in dirty weather was a rotten job, dashed uncomfortable, monotonous too, although I suppose there was

always the possibility of spotting something and
having a chase after it. They did their job well,
no doubt about that; for four years those leave
boats went to and from the Channel, every day,
without the loss of a single life.

At Boulogne everyone mechanically collected
their belongings, all wearing the 'fed up' look, and
it was a motley crowd of humanity that lined up
at the R.T.O.'s office. We were sent to the
A.M.L.O.'s to get orders, only to find he was busy
and we'd have to return later. He informed us
then that Brooky was posted to 101 Squadron at
St. Omer, and my destination was 100 Squadron
at Ochey, twenty-seven kilometres from Nancy and
away down in the Vosges district. We had hoped
to be sent to the same Squadron, and this proved
a great disappointment.

The route to Ochey was via Paris, and the train
left at 9 p.m., some three hours before the one for
St. Omer, so Brooky saw me aboard. Having
been together for over a year, we had a great
regard for each other, and an affection, such as a
man holds for his friend, had sprung up between
us. We had had many happy times too, but here
we had to part and wished each other "Good
luck."

Paris, reached the following morning, had no
fascination for me. All I wanted now was something to do, and the sooner the better. Kull, a
Flying Corps wireless expert on his way to Italy,
suggested the Hotel Continental for breakfast, and
it certainly came up to expectations. After a meal

and a bath, we popped into the toilet salon for a
shampoo. Jove, these French people certainly knew
how to attend to one's toilet, and the shampoo was
a treat. Then a petite female wanted to manicure
our finger-nails. I'd never let vanity get the upper
hand of me before, but this was different, and no
man could refuse to have such a chic little bit of
goods fiddling round him. We spent an hour or
more there, but drew the line when she wanted to
do our toe-nails. Even without that luxury, our
bill was twenty-eight francs, and although an
expensive hour, we stepped out feeling much refreshed.

The train for Nancy left the Gare de L'est at
mid-day, and I had already reserved a seat and
collected my traps from the Gare du Nord, so
with Kull went for a jolt around the city in one of
the antiquated taxis, had a peep at the Bastille,
Arc de Triomphe, and just had time to try one of
the famous champagne cocktails at Ciros. Good
job we had to go then, for the ladies were beginning to arrive, and the old nigger at the door
greeted them with a grin from ear to ear. He
evidently knew all their painted faces, and no
wonder, for they turned up regularly every day.
We got the glad eye from several directions, but
discreetly retired. We had neither the time nor
the inclination.

The same night, somewhere round about midnight, a railway official suddenly wakened me and
started to go off the deep end. Eventually I 'com-
pried.' We were some five miles from Nancy and

the train was going no further owing to the presence of enemy raiders.

"Well, all right, I'll stay here," I told him.

"But no, you cannot do that, you must get out and walk," he said.

"That be hanged for a yarn," I replied, "I'm a passenger to Nancy," but it was of no avail, out I had to get and fumble along the best way I could in the darkness. Stumbling along the lines, I finished up by sprawling full length over some signal wires, and cursed the War, the enemy, and all idiotic Frenchmen within hearing. Strangely enough, there seemed to be no other troops alighting, and as I lay there alone in the blackness, the humour of the situation suddenly struck me and I laughed. I got up and then sat down on my suitcase, which was lying by the rails, laughed again and remembered there was a war going on somewhere and I was on my way to it.

By this time, I could hear a booming, and reports at frequent intervals, reminding me of the reason for the train stoppage. The enemy airmen were visiting Nancy again, and I asked myself what I was going to do. No good sitting here, so I struck many matches, and after a good deal of fumbling around, found a road. This was better, but which way should I go? I stood there cogitating, when I thought I heard a vehicle approaching, and hailing it, found it was a French motor lorry. Yes, he was going into Nancy and would give me a lift certainly, he said, and I was told to hop into the back seat. A quarter of an hour later, I made my first entry into Nancy sitting on the tailboard of a motor lorry.

There was not a sign of life anywhere and everything was still dark, the enemy airmen having returned to their own side by now. The lorry driver suggested that I should endeavour to rouse the proprietor of the Hotel L'Angleterre, opposite the station. I thanked him, although I didn't agree that the said proprietor would need much waking, as the building next to him had had its front completely blown away by a bomb. The station had also been a target for two more bombs, and although there was just a possibility he might have slept through it, I hardly thought so.

I endeavoured to gain admittance by banging on the door, and daylight saw me still trying. He wasn't asleep, but was too scared to move. The Nancy folk had been through an exceedingly trying time, the town being a regular target for the Hun airmen.

When I was eventually allowed into the hotel, my host was hospitality itself, and I was grateful after the somewhat disturbing night.

When joining up with a new Squadron, one is naturally curious as to who's in it, and that is how I felt while awaiting the arrival of the tender that was to fetch me from Nancy. The same feeling was apparently at the aerodrome too, although not on my account, for the same tender was bringing the mails, and who should step out of the orderly room when we arrived but my old operation observer, Reid. He nearly fell on my neck with surprise.

"Jove, Bow, it's good to see you again," he said. "Come to join the happy family?"

"I suppose so," I muttered. "How long have you been here?"

"Three months," he told me.

"Anyone else here I know?"

"Sure, there's Lucas, Tatham, Albu, Windsor; he got the M.C., did you know? Miles is here too, great show this," Reid rambled off.

"Should think so, by the looks of it," I said, as my eye wandered from one bomb hole to another, then to the remains of a hangar.

"I note you have dug-outs," I remarked.

"Too right, and you darn well want 'em too. Let's go and find the rest of the boys," and he dragged me across to the mess.

It looked comfy enough. In the middle of the ante-room was a brazier, a big open-work basket of wrought iron, holding a huge, cheery wood fire. On a corner table was a phonograph, apparently suffering badly with asthma, judging by the wheezing noise it made, the walls were adorned with cuttings from illustrated papers, while over in the far corner stood a piano, minus one caster, judging by its tilt.

Two or three of the fellows were reading round the fire, while at a couple of small tables card games were in progress. It impressed me more favourably than I had expected, and everyone looked up as we entered. The next minute, I found myself trying to shake hands with half a dozen at once. This was great; I seemed to know most of them. There was Albu, an old Flight Commander of mine, who had previously had something to do with diamonds in Africa. Tatham, the six-footer, who used to rest his chin on his knees in the front seat of the old Fee—too much leg. Windsor, complete with M.C., who still wore the same grin, while poor old Lucas was looking just as worried as he always did in Blighty. He was still the fair-haired boy from Canada, hadn't gone grey yet. Miles hadn't altered a bit, still as mad as ever on poker. He and I had some good goes.

I was introduced all round. There was Alec Ward, an Aussie with no nerves. He was the bird the Huns said knocked the chimney tops off flying over Thionville one night, got the M.C., then went home and was killed in England. Billy Barnes, who went over as many times as anyone and did some great bombing. Little Box, who was so tiny that he had to have stilts to reach the rudder bar. His only fault was that he was too keen, got the D.F.C. and then was killed, crashed on our side. Hughie Chambers, he was a quiet one, liked climbing mountains better than flying; it was his pet hobby in New Zealand. Crofts had only just left school, mad as a hatter, didn't mind bombing, but didn't like being bombed. He celebrated his twentieth birthday soon after my arrival. Dear old Dad Crystall was the E.O. who fathered all the boys. Edwards Evans, who showed me the way first time over, had been in the Infantry, got the M.C., and was a good man to have in the front seat. Big Bill Rutherford, who tried to train a seven-a-side moustache, I mean it was a horrible failure, made good ballast for any machine. Darby was from the 'Hielands,' the solemn, gloomy one, full of dry wit, pulled off the D.F.C.

While the introductions were going forward, the C.O. entered, the D.S.O. and M.C. below his wings catching my eye immediately. Reid introduced me —Major Tempest—seemed very young to be C.O., certainly not more than 24. I was full of curiosity, so I asked Reid:

"Is he Tempest of the Zeppelin fame?"

"The same fellow," he informed me. "You've come to some flash Squadron, my boy, but let's have a drink to christen you." He pressed the tit, as he put it, and a corporal appeared. This was Minns, so I was told, came from Oxford, big chief drinks, and his tunic certainly looked it, couldn't see the cloth for splashes. I noticed it was also necessary for him to leave the two bottom buttons undone.

It was Minns who brought the drinks, Minns who waited at table, Minns who brought the breakfast in bed and collected half a franc for bringing it, Minns, who cleaned the boots, made the beds, in fact, Minns did this and Minns did that, and there was nothing Minns didn't do. It was also Minns who led the crowd to the dug-out, at the double too, when the alarms went, yet through it all his ruddy face was always beaming.

There was a happy crowd at dinner that night. The wash-out had been given, no flying, weather too bad. At midnight, poker was still going strong, and my new home had certainly impressed me favourably. It was like old times among all the old boys, they were a good mob, mostly youngsters, game for anything, at any time, as it was proved later.

Ochey aerodrome was situated on a slight rise, the only obstacles were the hangars. Those occupied by a naval squadron and our own three were on one side, while at the top end were several used by a French Squadron. On the far side of the landing ground was Ochey village itself, containing not more than thirty or forty houses. The surrounding country was hilly, and thickly wooded in many places, not too good for forced landings at night.

A little to the north-west was the town of Toul, a military centre, with quaint, cobbled streets and old-fashioned shops, which gave an antique appearance. Its Cathedral was a beautiful building of uncommon design, while the interior was a cause for marvel to the sightseer. This quaint little town stood in the shade of the twin mountains of St. Michel, while the Moselle River ran around the outskirts, both good landmarks for fliers.

To the N.E.E. was Pont St. Vincent, a fair-sized town on the Moselle River. Like Nancy, this place was a target for many Hun bombs, the steel works being the attraction.

From the line, our aerodrome was roughly twenty to thirty minutes' flying, and lighthouses served as guides at night, signalling letters in Morse. D and C were between the landing ground and the line, whilst others were placed east and west. The idea was good and enabled us to find our way home on many a dark night.

100 Squadron was the senior night flying squadron in France and was a unit of the Independent Air Force, whose job was reprisals.

Our authorities decided to give Fritz what he was giving us, and for every raid he carried out on England, we did at least six into his territory, and as time showed, he didn't like it.

Our targets were mostly in Alsace Lorraine, Metz, Diedenhofen, Trier, Saarbrucken on the Saar Valley, Kreuzwald, Courcelles and Conflans, enemy troops being in all these towns, as well as anything of military importance, and later we gave many of his aerodromes a good smack up.

The Day Squadron, flying D.H.4's, did as far as Cologne, and a darned good show too. The Naval Squadron went a bit farther than we did. They had Handleys, but didn't seem to do a lot of flying.

Alsace Lorraine was hard country for night fliers, and if it hadn't been for the rivers and woods, whose shapes we learnt to know by heart and which could always be discerned in the darkness, we would have been lost many a time. The blast furnaces of the steel works often aided us too, as their reflections could be seen for miles, although, after a time, they managed to keep these completely under control. Targets were hard to find on dark nights, compass courses would have to be followed, although it was difficult to allow for the drift. There were no drift instruments then, and coming home was harder than going, until you sighted a lighthouse, and the familiar . . of C was always welcome.

F.E.2.B. 5564 was alloted to me. I'd hoped for a better type of machine, although these old Fees did some great showing, carrying heavy loads of bombs night after night many miles into Hun territory. A four to five hour show in those days was an accomplishment, but it was done.

My first overseas flight was to get an idea of the country. I went alone in daylight, travelling eastward until Luneville was sighted. This town was only a matter of eight or ten miles from the line and had already been well shelled. The ruins and debris of many a fine old chateau could be discerned as one flew over. Following the line along, we crossed the Moselle at Pont a Mousson. This town was practically on the line, and a mass of ruins, not a house standing. The whole surrounding country was shelled, and as far as St. Michel Salient, the chalky lines of the trenches could be picked out quite easily. Just at that time, that particular part of the line was fairly quiet, save for the occasional burst of a shell, throwing clouds of earth into the air.

One could scarcely distinguish the lakes around Boncouville from the huge shell holes filled with water. Passing these, we flew over the Meuse River, and turned our backs on Verdun. On the roads, dotted here and there, troops and transport could be seen making for the line. It was whilst watching some of these troops from an altitude of four thousand that I received a terrific surprise. A small scout machine flashed past me at an enormous speed. I tried to get a look at him, but he was then above and behind me. The top of my head felt frozen and my hair stuck up so much that it nearly knocked my flying cap off, and I felt goosey all over. My first thought was, "It's a Hun," and I expected every second to hear the rat-tat-tat of a machine gun. Swinging the plane round, I tried to get a peep at him, and next minute he was alongside, enabling me to see the blue, red and white on his tail. It was just an inquisitive French Spad, wanting to have a good look at us. He waved, did a roll and went, but I couldn't help thinking what cold meat I'd have been had it turned out a Hun. The Fees were only night fliers and it was asking for a hurried exit out of this world, buzzing around the line in broad daylight. It was mid-winter and I was beginning to feel frozen. It started to snow a bit, so I stuck her nose down a little and headed for Ochey.

The snow lasted for a week-end everyone got pretty well fed up. It was as cold as charity everywhere except around the old brazier, where we warmed our knees hour after hour. Someone suggested a wood-cutting parade, anything to relieve the monotony, so we got a tender and went to the Forest de Haye, where axes and saws made the blood circulate once more.

When we did take the air next time, the whole country was a picture, with its mantle of snow. It

seemed to blot out all the destruction of war.
There was no show this night, weather too un-
settled, but Swart, another new pilot from the same
country as Albu, and myself, were ordered up to
go the round of the lighthouses. It was a perfect
starlit night when we left and I enjoyed it. After
climbing two thousand feet, I could see D Lighthouse twinkling away some nineteen kilos off. I
made for it, and then on to C, three miles from
the line, down to B, skirting Nancy, and not
desirous of getting mixed up in any balloon barrage, I turned back. About five miles from the
aerodrome, I picked up the navigation lights of
Swart's bus, coming from the opposite direction.
He signalled that he was going to land, I acknow-
ledged it and followed him. We had been away
an hour, and not five minutes after our return it
commenced to snow again, which stopped the flying
for several days.

Swart and I were keen for the weather to clear,
as the C.O. had told us we could go up on the next
show, Edwards Evans being picked for my observer. Each evening the weather report would
come through and we would dash off to read it, but
always with the same result, 'Dud.' Eventually,
however, the weather showed signs of improve-
ment, and on the night of February ninth, we had
the immense pleasure of unloading four nice large
bombs and several drums of ammunition on the
enemy. Operation orders read—'Objective Courcelles Railway Junction—bombs 112 and 230 poun-
ders. A Flight will lead.'

It is difficult to describe your feelings the first night going over the enemy's lines. I was eaten up with curiosity, anxious to put up a good show, yet not knowing quite what to expect. Old pilots had given advice not to take unnecessary risks, not to come down too low on a first flight to do your bombing, remember to switch off your navigation lights before going on the line, and I found their advice useful.

The night of February ninth was just as dark and cold as it could be, and in spite of thigh boots, fur coat and many other accessories, we literally froze.

At six p.m. there was activity everywhere at the aerodrome. Flares were out, mechanics dashing here and there, machines lined up, and punctually at that hour, Swart and I were strolling with the rest up to our own machines. It was to be our christening, so we shook hands and wished each other "Good luck." That was the last time I saw Swart, he spent the remainder of his war days in a Hun prison camp.

Edwards Evans and I inspected the bombs, parachute flare, wingtip flares and all the rest of the gadgets, then climbed into our seats. The mechanic was ready at the engine.

"Switches off, Sir," he shouted.

"Switches off," I replied, "Suck in," and he swung the propeller round a few times.

"Switch on, Sir," he yelled. I twisted the C.A.V. and away went the prop. at thirteen hundred revolutions to the minute. We let the engine

warm up and then tried her full out, O.K., and
waited for the signal to go.

Our Flight Commander was leading, he taxied
out and we were signalled to follow. Swinging
her round into the flare path, I pushed the throttle
forward and away we went, skimming on what
was my first raid of destruction over enemy lines.
The plane climbed into the darkness, and at three
hundred feet we turned. Another machine was
just leaving and I watched him as he roared down
the flare path, the red-hot exhaust showing clearly
in the inky blackness of the night. The first
machine to leave was just above us. We circled
the aerodrome once and then left at eight hundred
feet. The tail light of the first bus showed plainly
and I followed it in the direction of D Lighthouse,
then turning slightly to the right, headed for C.
Looking back, I could still see the lights of the
other four machines following. B and C Flights
were to leave at ten minute intervals. At C Lighthouse, I switched off our light and set on course
N.N.W. Our target was roughly forty minutes'
flying from the line and we crossed this at three
thousand feet.

We were now over enemy territory.

"Keep your eyes skinned," my observer leant
over and yelled to me.

"Can't see a damned thing," I replied, and there
was not a light to be seen anywhere, just blank,
impenetrable darkness, broken only by the red
glare of the exhaust and the glow of the dash-
board.

Keeping her nose to the N.N.W. for twenty minutes, I peered over the side to try and distinguish something that might serve to assure us that we were on the right course, but the density of the night gave no sign, except the whistling of the wind as we speeded by. The drone of the engine kept us company, purr, purr, it was running perfectly. We were doing seventy miles an hour at twelve hundred revolutions. We flew on, keeping at three thousand feet; fifteen to twenty minutes more would find us very near our target. In spite of warm clothing and the usual thigh boots, I was getting cold, the bitter stinging of the keen wind making my face tingle. My observer was well hidden in his seat, the only part showing occasionally being his head popping up above the nacelle.

Suddenly the monotony was broken, and I could see my observer leaning over the side, hand on machine gun. Every part of the machine was plainly visible. A searchlight had pierced the darkness and caught us first go. He was directly to the left. Evans stood up, both hands grasping the gun, and signalled to swing round. Kicking the rudder and pulling the joy stick over, I throttled back and dived straight down the beam. The machine gun spit forth, a burst of ten or so, but he didn't shut down. I side-slipped and he lost us. We were now at eighteen hundred feet and he was hunting the skies for us, found us for a second and then let us go again. We turned and throttled back once more, taking another dive at him.

Coming down to one thousand feet, Evans gave two or three good bursts; he immediately switched off and did not light up again. Eventually we picked up our course and proceeded undisturbed. The excitement had warmed us, or else we had forgotten the cold.

Ten minutes passed and I consulted my map, which showed that we should be within five miles. Evans leant over.

"Can't be far off," he yelled.

"About five miles, I reckon. Keep your eyes open for Windsor's phosphorous bomb," I replied. The leader on dark nights carried a phosphorous bomb, which usually set fire to something and lit up the surroundings. Our instructions were to drop our bombs as near this signal as possible.

Evans had scarcely reseated himself when, over to our right, not more than two miles away, we saw this bomb burst and light up the surroundings. It must have been seen for miles, and we immediately swung around and made for it. Approaching and keyed up with excitement as we were, we saw another burst, then three in quick succession and only a few yards apart. It was good bombing and the five made an excellent group. The first had caused a fire and we flew round once to have a look, discerning a group of buildings. Guiding the plane over them, Evans let two go and the bursts were quite visible, close together. We turned back and he let drop the others. Looking down to watch the effect, another searchlight caught us, and realising that the place was well protected against aircraft raids, I turned to dodge him, and instinctively looking over the side, I noticed a whole string of machine gun fire making directly for us. Like a procession of glow-worms these phosphorous bullets approached, and I immediately turned the plane in the opposite direction, dodging one searchlight but running into another line of machine gun fire. We'd dropped all our bombs, so I turned her nose down and beat it. We ended up at eight hundred feet and headed for C Lighthouse. We'd stirred up a hornets' nest and we felt that some of the machines to come after us would have a pretty hot time.

Looking back, we could see searchlights busy and bombs dropping everywhere. A good strafe was in progress and we pitied the last poor devil, for he'd get it hot and strong. Our chief concern at that moment, however, was to get back, and the night was still black. Evans was itching to use his gun, but no more searchlights showed up and nothing could be seen. We flew on through the night, the engine purring away in good style, and the excitement of the raid wearing off somewhat, we began to feel the intense cold again. That lighthouse seemed a long way off, no sign of it yet. I looked at the compass and it showed us in the right course; time we picked up the light and we tried to pierce the darkness, but without avail. Surely we must be off our course. There must be a bit of a drift, nothing to take our bearings on, and we swung the plane a little to the south. Our eyes were aching with the strain and I closed mine for a second or two, raising my goggles, and feeling instant relief.

Then, away to the left, a tiny speck of light caught my eye, seeming to stand out in the darkness, although no twinkle was visible. At any rate, we swung around in that direction and I yelled out to ask Evans what he could make of it.

"Can't say, but go that way," he called back. We both glued our eyes to the tiny speck, our hearts full of hope, and the next moment I could have sworn that it flashed a signal . . Evans leant over again and shouted:

"That's it all right—put it here," and we shook hands away up at three thousand feet. Nothing more was said, but we each realised the other's feelings of relief that we were safely back on our own side of the line. In a short twenty minutes or so, my first raid over Hunland would be over. We'd been lucky though, picking up the lighthouse —a few minutes more and we should have passed it for we were quite fifteen miles out of our course. This verified my suspicions of drift, there must have been a fair wind. A short time after passing the lighthouse, the landing flares could be seen plainly and my whole body seemed to relax its nervous tension. A feeling of complete satisfaction set in, and just then a French anti-aircraft battery challenged us, reminding me that I'd completely forgotten to switch on the navigation lights. He challenged us again and I fired a Very light colour of the night and he was satisfied. Throttling back as we neared the aerodrome, I signalled my desire to land. The spotlights were switched on and next minute we swung into view. Our wheels touched earth, we taxied to the hangar, switched off and climbed from our seats. The first thing I did was to grope for my cigarettes, congratulations were extended and I felt very bucked, safely back after my first show.

Only one other machine had landed, although we could see lights from three others. Evans and I went to the orderly room, made out our report and handed it in to the C.O., who seemed very pleased. After all, it wasn't a particularly good night.

We next made tracks for the mess, to get a spot and celebrate the occasion. Discarding some of our heaviest garments, we strolled back to the hangars to find out how the others had fared. Fourteen out of eighteen machines had landed, groups of men stood here and there, chatting over the events of the trip. They had all found the searchlights troublesome and the machine gun fire hot. Miles got a strut shot through and one of his bombs failed to explode, which annoyed him. He delighted in serving out this destruction. Barnes declared it took a whole damn drum to shut up one searchlight which was particularly troublesome, and he seemed to begrudge the ammunition. Big Bill's only growl was that he couldn't see a damn thing. Like us, they had all found the drift.

At this juncture, two machines appeared, only two more to come. A few minutes passed and one more showed up. It turned out to be Little Box, and he'd had engine trouble all the way, so much so that he doubted if he'd ever see the aerodrome again.

Still one more plane to come, who was it? The question went round.

"All B and C Flight are back, Sir," a mechanic informed us. Well, who's missing from A? Windsor, Crofts, Miles, Martin, Kingsford, all back. It's Swart. We strained our eyes in the direction of the line, but no machine lights could be seen. I remembered how keen he was and how we had talked of what we hoped to do on our first show. He was determined to put up a good performance and I wondered if he had been tempted to get down too low and so caught some of those tracer bullets. We hung about until we knew his benzine must be exhausted and that he must be down somewhere, and not until then did we think of returning to the mess.

There was no jubilation and one by one we crept to our huts, after a final look to see if the missing machine had turned up.

At that time, Swart and his observer, Fielding-Clarke, were down in Hunland, groping around in the darkness: their engine having failed them and so forced them to land near the line. They were not sure which side they were on, as a matter of fact, but received a nasty shock when four of the enemy appeared on the scene. Swart's first show was his last—Karlsruhe Prison Camp claimed him.

The British Official Report of this raid is appended:—

"On Saturday night, our night bombing machines carried out a successful raid into Germany, although the weather was by no means good.

Nearly a ton of bombs was dropped, with very good results, on the important railway junction and siding at Courcelles-les-Metz (S.E. of Metz). One of our bombing machines is missing."

CHAPTER VII

REPRISALS

FOR some time now the weather was good, and raids were numerous. Often we would make two journeys a night into Hunland, perhaps crawling home just at dawn, pretty fatigued. We felt the cold terribly, especially on the long shows. 1917-18 was a severe winter in the Vosges.

Metz was often raided, a short show, only twenty-five miles over the lines, but a hot shop nevertheless. There were plenty of aircraft batteries, machine guns, balloon barrage. The last-named were rotten things, forming a circle round the town with balloons and suspending nets between them. You never knew what height you were safe to fly at. There were flaming onions too, coming up at us by the dozen, and consisting of a sort of fire-ball, specially designed to ignite anything they came in contact with, particularly benzine and aeroplanes. They were slow travelling, however, and we usually managed to dodge them.

Metz was a very important enemy position, the whole of the Verdun front being fed by the railways passing through this junction. Many a time we disorganised things and did tremendous damage by consistently bombing this stronghold. The enemy cursed us, not only for the damage and disorganisation, but for the moral effect that was telling on their troops.

Diedenhofen was a favourite target of ours and was situated some twenty-five miles further on from Metz. Like the latter, it was a hard show, plenty of defence and containing another important railway junction. There were also important steel works, and we let go numbers of bombs on them. Our planes only averaged sixty miles an hour and it often meant a very uncomfortable two hour trip to Diedenhofen.

Treves (Trier) was our longest show, forty odd miles beyond Diedenhofen, and roughly ninety miles over the lines. We could only carry a light load of bombs for this trip, owing to the quantity of benzine necessary. The journey took roughly four and a half to five hours, and extra tanks had to be added. Even then, we could only just get back with sufficient, provided there were no contrary head winds. Treves had large army barracks, which was our objective, and we carried out more than one raid on these. Considering the old type of machine and the distance covered, it was a great demonstration of what could be done.

Conflans, Courcelles, Hagending, Mazieres, all were raided in turn, in addition to the electric power stations at Kreuzwald, which supplied the famous forts at Metz with electricity, light and power. This was a particularly hard place to find,

being right among the forests of Alsace Lorraine
and surrounded by hilly country. Even in moon-
light, when raids here had to be carried out, it
could easily be missed.

We had casualties of course; Taylor, Le Feurve,
Reid, Fielding-Clarke, Jackson, went missing.
Albu, Lindsay, Parnell and Tatham crashed. Poor
old Tat was pretty badly knocked out, chest crushed.
Albu got nervy and didn't fly again.

On the night of February 26-27, we raided Frescaty aerodrome, just south of Metz. We left the
ground at six twenty p.m., taking off without
lights, for we were expecting a visit from the
enemy airmen and our C.O. very wisely ordered
us up earlier than usual, considering it safer for
us to be in the air rather than on the aerodrome.
As it happened, however, the enemy were concentrating on Nancy that night, and we saw his handiwork going on as we passed. Bombs were exploding,
anti-aircraft shells were bursting and searchlights
were busy. Presuming that the enemy had come
from Frescaty, we hung about the line for a while
before crossing, hoping to catch him when he lit
up for landing.

Following the Moselle River northwards, we
found the target without trouble, the Zeppelin shed
stood out plainly, as well as the wood where the
hangars were concealed. We circled round for a
bit, hoping something would happen, but in the end
the searchlights got too troublesome and we were
forced to let go our pills. The first two exploded
between the hangars and the remainder on huts.

8

There must have been almost a dozen searchlights after us, and flaming onions were coming up from all directions. The occasional 'woof' of exploding 'archie' shells reminded us that enemy gunners were on our trail. It was the finest firework display that I'd ever seen, although I would have preferred viewing it from a safer distance.

The mist of a rising moon in our faces made the return journey difficult. Johnson, Miles and Naylor were missing, but telephoned early in the morning to say that they had overshot the aerodrome in the mist and had landed at Tantonville, away down by Vezelise. Our anxiety was greatly relieved by this news.

A second raid was to be carried out that night, and preparations were in progress when a nasty accident occurred. One of our bombs exploded, killing poor old Scuds, a Flight Sergeant, and three other men. The infernal thing had failed to leave the carrier in the first raid and an examination was being carried out when it happened. These bombs had a small propeller, which revolved twenty-five times before the firing pin was opposite the detonator. As the bomb left the carrier, the propeller revolved and exploded on striking earth. As a safety device, a pin was always on the carrier preventing the propeller from revolving while the bomb was in the carrier. Apparently this bomb had partly dropped below the pin, just sufficient to allow the propeller to revolve, and the bomb had lowered while the inspection was on. The poor chaps were close beside and received the full force of the explosion. It put a damper on things, and the C.O. 'washed out' for that night. Scuds was a popular observer and had just got the M.C. Those decorations were fatal things.

After the Frescaty show, a new machine was allotted to me, an F.E.2.C., designed much the same as a B, but the pilot sat in front. They were more comfortable and there was plenty of room for long-legged fellows like myself. My observer and I were delighted and set to work to make some improvements. We painted her black like the other machines and designed the skull and cross-bones on her nose. She was faster than 2 B and more sensitive on controls. 'Smuts,' my prehistoric-looking mascot, with the perpetual grin from ear to ear, was given a place of honour, and we wired him to the instrument board.

We tested her again and again and found everything O.K., looking forward with eagerness to the next show. We were anxious to know what we could do on a machine that was as good as possible. But she failed us horribly the very first night, the engine cutting out at fifty feet. She picked up again and then faded clean away, and we landed, in great disgust, to the sound of a burst tyre. We were forced to take another machine that night, although the following day we could find nothing wrong with the engine and never had any more trouble. I flew her for months until I had a final smash up. Funny how these engines behave sometimes; like the weaker sex, one never knows just how to take them.

The enemy was evidently getting fed up with our bombing, and he tried to quieten us by concentrating on our aerodrome. Every fine night during the following month he paid us a visit, and although some dozens of bombs were dropped, he never did any great damage. It only caused us inconvenience. An empty hangar was hit one night and there were several pot-holes in the landing ground.

Our C.O. was full of ideas and we did not stay there long. We deceived the Hun airmen for a long time before they discovered our whereabouts. Not a mile from the landing ground were the Ochey Woods, and we camouflaged new hangars and huts, made a good runaway, and lived in perfect serenity. We used to watch him at night, bombing our old aerodrome, where we had left the hangars and rigged up necessary gear to cause a fire by the mere pressing of a button from our grand stand. Fritz would appear, drop a few bombs, our button would be pressed, a fire would light up, and some lucky enemy airman would get the Iron Cross next morning. Then over would come the enemy daylight machines to take photographs, and we did our best to assist them by posing some old scrapped machine, often more than one, on the landing ground near a bomb hole, thus verifying the previous night's work. More Iron Crosses would be handed round.

But as time wore on, Fritz could not understand why we could continue raiding his towns and military centres. He wondered how we could carry

on if his raids were so successful as pictured. We
certainly never missed an opportunity, two shows
a night, often eighteen machines; he was mystified.
Soon after this, more daylight machines came over
to know the cause, and it was not until new tracks
began to show up on the landing ground of our
fresh aerodrome that he discovered where we were.
Then he let us have it, but did no real damage.
His bombing was only fair.

There were certainly times when he proved a
great nuisance though. I remember one night,
returning from a long raid, benzine almost finished
and all lights out at the aerodrome, showing us
that raiders were about. We signalled our desire
to land and received no reply. The landing lights
were not switched on and we had no alternative
but to float around for a bit, repeating our request
to land at frequent intervals. There must have
been a dozen or so of us signalling away up there.
Round and round we went, and how on earth there
was not a collision was a mystery to me. It was
dark and we expected our benzine to fizzle out at
any moment. In the end, I decided to land in the
darkness, thinking I knew pretty well every bump
on the runaway. We were making our final circuit
before coming in, when the engine spat and splut-
tered and konked right out. Our altitude was only
two hundred feet, so I stuck on the wing tip flares,
gazing ahead and below and discerning nothing but
woods. Suddenly my observer yelled:

"Look out!" and I saw that we were flying
clean into a row of poplars so familiar in France.

The machine had enough speed for me to zoom over them, then pushing her nose down, I spotted a clear space and flattened out for landing. I heard a swishing as though something was skimming the lower plane and then she stopped dead. We had landed in a wheat field, with a crop some four feet high. All the boys got down that night without crashing, but were not so fortunate a couple of nights later.

When returning from Saarbrucken, we floated round for half an hour until, some distance away, brilliant lights were switched on into the darkness. We went over to investigate and found it was a landing ground all right. There was a straight row of lights and I was not certain whether to land parallel to them or not. We were accustomed to lights placed in the form of a letter L and landing parallel to the long arm. I counted five other machines, navigation lights on, flitting round having a look the same as we were. I decided to wait until one landed to see which way he came in. It was quite a while before anyone attempted it, and I noticed he came in over the lights. I watched him closely, saw him touch ground O.K., run a little and then turn turtle and disappear from sight. Apparently that was the wrong way, so I decided to try something different. We managed to get down all right, but overshot and just escaped running into a hill. In swinging round to avoid a bump, we contrived to tear a wheel off.

It was Barnes whom I had seen turn turtle; he had apparently run down a steep slope. Crofts did the same and smashed things up. Miles followed suit, but no one was seriously hurt. All this happened at Epiez, a French aerodrome, and badly situated especially when you didn't know the place.

The French treated us well, supplied us with a car, and we reached Ochey at three a.m. to find things pretty well upside down. Fellows had landed all over the country and the enemy had given the aerodrome fellows a pretty warm time. While no great damage was done, bombs had fallen in a few inconvenient places, one being just outside our hut. The interior was thrown into a confused mass, things all over the show and all mixed up together. We sifted it all out by daylight, and no one had any sleep until the next night. It was verging on a nightmare.

Those of us who had managed to land at Epiez without altogether smashing our machines, attempted to return to do a raid from there. During the raid, the driver of our tender had been injured and some other A.M. offered to drive us over. It was only a distance of some twenty miles, but we had some fun.

The volunteer couldn't drive, so McCreath had a go, proving worse still. Passing through one village, we ran into a herd of cows. One got hit and was slow to move, so McCreath gave it a bump; the cow immediately mounted the car, ending up with its hind legs astride the bonnet and front legs on the ground. It did its best to trot along with the car until McCreath managed to direct it straight into a manure heap in front of a house, and there it stopped. We all got out then and assisted the cow to dismount, afterwards all taking a turn at the wheel. We found, however, that the volunteer was the best of a bad bunch, so the car was given back to his charge and everything went all right until we were within five miles of the aerodrome.

We were on a long, straight road, running through an avenue of poplars, with a ten-foot drop on either side, when we met a large timber, horse-drawn wagon. These wagons were very wide and we all knew, long before we reached it, that we would hit it. It did not come as a very great surprise, therefore, when, after almost passing it, the back wheels of both vehicles clashed, and the next second we were all over the bank, a small mass of struggling humanity. The tender turned a somersault, pinning two or three of us underneath. There had been fourteen before we went over the bank, and when we came to sort ourselves out, everyone was there O.K. except Harper, McCreath, Jock Henry and myself. We were taken to a charming chateau, where we remained for the night, being taken off next day by ambulance to an American hospital. Harper and McCreath were admitted, while Jock and I returned to our Squadron, feeling A1 after a few days.

We were the only British troops in this sector, and about this time the American army arrived and made its headquarters at Neuf Chateau, a few miles south of us. We welcomed other troops who spoke our language, and they came up in hundreds to see us. Very few of them had seen an aeroplane before and were as keen as mustard. They all wanted a flip, and if a fellow happened to be out testing his machine, he was besieged on all sides. Questions were hurled out by the dozen; their ignorance was astounding, even on ordinary things pertaining to aviation. They were thirsting for information and we made many friends among them. What amused us was the number of motor cars they brought with them. Their transport park was simply enormous and every Yankee private seemed to have brought his own car with him. They were generous with them too, and if we were ever stuck for transport, we had only to ring up and state our needs.

Following the arrival of the Yanks, some Italians appeared, complete with 'Caproni's.' These machines were considered the very latest in bombers, having three engines and carrying a crew of four, and being capable of doing long shows with heavy loads. Whether they were hard to handle or whether the pilots were only mediocre, I don't know, but they had plenty of crashes, and one bird wrote his machine off the first day they arrived. We helped to pick up the pieces.

A spell of bad weather suspended operations just at this time. Everywhere there was snow a foot deep, and the only place approaching warmth was in the mess. We didn't leave it more than we could help, except for a trip to Nancy for a good feed, and by way of breaking the monotony.

Irvine Cobb, the well-known American War

Correspondent, paid us a visit one night and was very disappointed because it was a 'dud' night and there were no shows on. We gave him an idea of night operations, however, by lighting the flares and a few of us going up, returning afterwards to the mess for the evening.

I always remember Irvine Cobb as one of those happy-go-lucky individuals, with a wonderful repertoire of stories, and he kept us going this night for a couple of hours or more. We finished up round the piano, yelling our heads off in the early hours of the morning. His report of the visit was published in the "Saturday Evening Post" of June 15th, 1918, and read:—

"For guests of honour there were four of us, and for hosts there were sixty to seventy members of Night Bombing Squadron No. 100.

It so happened that this particular group of young dare-devils represented every main division of the Empire's Domain, as we were told that there were Englishmen, Welshmen, Scots and Irishmen, also Canadians, Australians, New Zealanders, an Afrikander or two, a dark youngster from India, as well as recruits gathered from lesser lands and lesser colonies where the Union Jack floats in the seven seas that girdle the globe. We were introduced to a flyer bred and reared in Japan, who had hurried to the Mother Isle immediately he had reached the volunteer age, a shy, quiet lad, with a downy upper lip.

I took pains to ascertain the average age of
the personnel of the Squadron. I am giving no
information to the enemy that he does not already
know, to his cost, when I state it to be twenty-two
and a half years.

Well, we had dinner, but before, a thing befell
which to me was as simply dramatic as anything
could possibly be. Glasses had been charged all
round and we were standing to drink the toast
of the British Aviator, when a servant entered,
and handed the Squadron Commander a slip of
paper bearing a bulletin just received by telephone from Wing Headquarters. The young
Major read it through, silently at first, and then
aloud:—

    'Eight machines of Squadron 55 made a
    daylight raid this afternoon. The operations
    were successfully carried out (a little pause).
    Three machines "failed to return."'

Six men, mates of these youngsters assembled
here and friends to some of them, had gone
down in the wreckage of their aircraft, probably
to death, or to what was hardly less terrible than
death, captivity in a German Prison Camp.

Well, it was all in a day's work; no one spoke,
but the glasses came up with a jerk and we
drank the airman's toast, 'Happy Landings.' I
don't profess to speak for others, but for myself,
I know I drank to the memory of those six blithe

boys, riders in the three machines that 'failed to return' and to a happy landing for them in the eternity to which they had been hurried long before their time."

Concluding, Irvine Cobb says:—

"When next I passed by that road, the hangars were empty of life. The great offensive had started a week before and on the third day of it, as we learned from our sources, our friends of Squadron 100, obeying an order, had climbed into their planes in pairs and had gone winging away to do their share in the air fighting where the fighting lines were locked fast. There was need for every available British aeroplane, the more need because each day showed a steadily mounting list of lost machines and lost airmen. I doubt whether many of those blithesome lads came out of that hell alive and doubt very much, too, whether I shall ever see any of them again."

When Irvine Cobb passed the hangars on that occasion and found them empty, we were away at Villesneux, south of Rheims, at a new aerodrome, having left Ochey to take part in the big push.

CHAPTER VIII

EXIT F.E.2 C. 450

HAVE you ever been surrounded by champagne? Well, that was our experience soon after our removal to Villesneux. Our new quarters were situated just south of Rheims, the centre of the champagne industry, and the good French folks were generosity itself. Apparently they had reasons for being so, as prior to our arrival, the enemy had bombed Epernay, Chateau Thierry and the other important towns of the Marne, making things most unpleasant for the unfortunate inhabitants. Our appearance, however, directed the enemy's attention to another quarter of more military importance, thereby giving these poor folks a brief respite. In consequence we were hailed as something like heroes and our presence in the town seemed to be the signal for festivities. They lavished their best wines and champagnes upon us and we did not refuse, making the most of it while the going was good. We groped through the darkness of the underground vaults, feasting our eyes on the bottles of fizz stacked there, some of them half a century old, and we drank of the best. Old Monsieur LeLarge always said that if the cork swelled when he pulled it, the wine was no good and he would throw it away, but invariably the cork did not swell and we drank. Good old bubbly.

Johnnie got hopelessly stunned one night, wanted to bath in one of the big barrels; we told him he'd drown in his present state, but he said he'd risk it and that no one could desire a more glorious death. He had a different idea next morning, and half a dozen aspirins had no effect on his head.

But we had been sent up this way to work. The enemy was making his final effort and every available machine was wanted. He had to be held and repelled at all costs, so the champagne stunts were only events for the absolutely impossible flying nights.

Our eighteen machines were landed safely on the Villesneux landing ground one misty afternoon in the Spring, and without losing any time, we made ourselves acquainted with the landscape. A few formation flights by day and a couple of visits up the line at night were sufficient for us, and a week after our arrival we were going strong.

Behind the enemy's lines were scenes of great activity, thousands of troops, transport, batteries, etc. Most of these moved up to the line at night, and we were often given roving commissions, in other words, orders to bomb anything of military importance wherever activity could be seen. At other times, a definite target would be ordered, Juneville Railway Junction and Mohon being two important ones.

This sector was much easier for night flying, having better landmarks and enabling us to find our way with less difficulty, the Marne River and Rheims Cathedral being the outstanding guides. The magnificent Cathedral was our aid on many a dark night, the flames of destruction, which the enemy seemed to delight in keeping burning, shooting high into the sky and lighting our way for miles. We scarcely bothered about a map, except for targets, and this lighthouse never failed. Out of curiosity and strictly against orders, I flew over to it one night, my thankful feelings for its usefulness as a guide, mingled with sorrow, when I looked down on the beautiful edifice of bygone days blazing away into ruins, fresh sheets of flame appearing where the masonry crumbled away. It burnt for month after month.

Big game hunting has its thrills and so has night bombing, and one of our chief delights was train bombing. We got plenty of it too during our sojourn in this part of the line. The enemy kept their railways busy at night bringing up troops, ammunition, foodstuffs and other materials, so to us they were important targets, and roving commissions were wise orders.

Trains were sporting targets, however, and their destruction often had a far-reaching effect. On these raids we usually carried eight twenty pound bombs and one two-thirty pounder. Each of these bombs was capable of derailing a train. We also carried three drums of ammunition.

One clear, starlit night, we set off with a big

load and high hopes, making for our favourite hunting ground around Juneville. We kept at four thousand feet and circled round to watch and wait events. Nothing happened for half an hour and we were giving up hope when my observer spotted the familiar faint glow of an engine coming to a standstill. We made straight for it, throttling back and commencing to descend slowly. Apparently they were not aware of our presence, for they opened their furnace door, giving us the opportunity of seeing everything clearly. All excitement, we continued to descend and my observer was itching to let go. At two thousand feet, I cut the engine down completely, the propeller just tickling over, almost silent. We swung round on the tail of the train, continued straight on over it, and waving me a little to the left, Sawyer in the front seat let go two bombs together. We were now only twelve hundred feet and the explosion shook the plane violently. With engines once more full on, we climbed, turned again to get a glance at our handiwork, and could see smoke rising, although it was difficult to ascertain the extent of the damage. We came over the spot again, let go a flare, which hung in the air for several minutes, lighting up the surroundings, and watched intently, discerning, as it neared the earth, the wreckage of overturned carriages. Our bombs had done their work and we were satisfied to dart off in another direction, searching for fresh prey. Nothing much could be found, however, so we returned to the junction and let go the rest of our pills. Turning south, we took a last glance at the old Cathedral away on the horizon, and made for home.

Things at the mess were pretty willing. News had just come through that Bright Eyes, Little Box and Darby had been awarded D.F.C.'s. It was an occasion to be celebrated. Minns, the cocktail mixer, was ordered to bring out some fizz, and when all this had been used, we tried vin blanc, but they didn't mix too well and many of us suffered ill-effects.

At 2 a.m. Cherry Martin mounted his favourite seat on top of the piano and gave his stock solo, "A German Officer Crossed the Rhine—Parlez Vous!" to rounds of applause. He gave about twenty verses, and when he had finished, Crofts insisted on reciting "There was an old ram of Derbyshire." Some of the lines wouldn't bear repeating. After that he did some juggling with the crockery, which ended in a battle royal until Big Bill walked the table, upset it and landed on the floor, surrounded by the broken pieces. We eventually crawled to our huts about three o'clock in the morning and dug in.

The C.O., who had been conspicuous by his absence, decided about this time to look at the night, which was still clear and starlit. Feeling a bit sore over something, he decided that another show would do us good, and we got a rude awakening when the orderly paraded the huts, yelling:

"All pilots and observers out for a show!"

Lucas, who shared a room with me, snored on,

and it was in vain that I tried to wake him. We threw a bowl of cold water over him, but even then he wouldn't believe that a show was ordered, and absolutely refused to dress. In the end, he came up to the hangars in his pyjamas and an overcoat, and before he knew where he was, someone stuck a flying cap on his head and bundled him into the front seat. A few minutes later, he was fully awake, and shivered with the intense cold at a thousand feet up. He despatched all his bombs over at Mohon and lost no time in getting back 'toute suite.'

Our next stunt proved somewhat of a failure, not due to any fault of ours, but to that element with which we always had to contend, the weather. Orders had come through that the enemy was concentrating on Amiens and that we were to proceed at once to Arcy-St. Restitue, a French aerodrome south-west of Soissons. From there, we were to carry out a raid on Chaulnes Railway Junction, one of the main junctions supplying the needs of the enemy.

We left late in the afternoon, and most of us arrived just after dark. It was a difficult place to find and no flares were put out, in consequence of which some of the boys had extreme difficulty in locating the landing ground. Everyone arrived safely, however, and there were no crashes.

The weather turned very misty, necessitating the postponement of our raid for a while. It was no better at eleven o'clock, but the C.O. decided to send us in spite of it. My observer on this expedition was an enthusiastic mechanic, who seemed to bring bad luck to everyone he flew with. On this occasion I was first to take off, and was not well acquainted with the French method of laying out the landing lights. Someone had told me there would be three lights in the form of a triangle and that I should take off over the apex. The mist was so thick, however, that we all knew before leaving how impossible it would be to find the target, although we realised it was just a case of doing our damnedest. Away we went, my faithful old 2 C roaring down the flare path and taking off in good style, despite the extra heavy load. At twenty feet off the ground, however, I felt something hit the plane. I couldn't see anything or find out what was happening, until the machine suddenly got out of control and the left wing dipped. I looked over the side, and to my horror, by the glow from the wing tip navigation light, I could see that the lower plane was damaged and the whole leading edge was smashed in. One of the struts was hanging from the top plane and dangling about in the air. I pulled the joy stick over, but with no effect, and a sickening sensation came over me. Nothing could avoid a crash; we were falling like a stone in the misty darkness. I switched the engine off and waited for what seemed to me an age before the crash came. Then there was a thud and a crunch of splintering wood-work as the damaged wing folded up beneath us and the cockpit struck the earth, throwing me from the front seat sprawling on to the short, stiff stalks of newly-cut wheat, which were responsible for removing a good deal of skin from the exposed portions of my anatomy.

After fully realising that we had crashed, it dawned on me that I was not alone in this affair and that I had left the aerodrome with an enthusiastic observer. I groped around the machine, feeling in his seat, but couldn't find him. I called out, and a muffled sound came from the darkness. Going in the direction of the sound, I stumbled forward, down hill, and yelled again:

"Where are you?"

"Here," came the reply, "give us a hand, I'm in a blasted bog." Cautiously I went down and found him, up to his waist in water and trying to wipe the muck from his face. The humour of the situation suddenly struck me and I laughed. We were a bright-looking pair; there was he, complete with flying suit and smothered in mud, while I was half covered with mud and blood all over my face. I helped him out, narrowly avoiding slipping into the bog myself.

Daylight revealed my old 2 C a complete 'write off,' sitting on top of a small rise in the contour and just below the ditch, which had so willingly received my unfortunate observer. He never desired to fly after this.

But we were not alone in our crash that night, for Harper came down in the Forest of Compeigne and also wrote off his bus. Night flying might be safer in some ways, but a forced landing in the dark is not pleasant. The engine cuts out and you

simply have to get down the best way you can
without breaking your neck not knowing what is
underneath you. Give me day flying any time,
you can see what you're up to.

Some of the boys thought they found the target
that night, but the show was a wash-out on the
whole and everyone was disappointed. We were
fortunate in having no casualties, however.

Harper and I stayed behind next day to pick up
the remains of our machines, returning afterwards
to Villesneux by road, via Chateau Thierry. Little
did I think, passing through that delightful little
picturesque town on the Marne, that it would be
the scene of such violent fighting, leaving the Hun
in possession, as he was a few weeks later.

I was given a new machine, F.E.2 B 5625.

A run of bad luck followed this show, Ford and
Collins both crashing and being killed. We buried
them at the American Military Cemetery at Vitry
Le Francois. Then dear old Bow Sawyer got
pneumonia and died. He'd served before the masts
of the good old sailing ships, hard as nails, yet
fate decided he should go thus. He was much
missed. On top of that, Andy and O'Connor were
reported missing.

Andy was a curly-headed Canadian, mad as they
make 'em, did some great shows too, yet in the air
he never knew where he was. He just flew and
relied on his observer to find the way. He got lost
one night, flying on a reconnaissance in England,
saw some landing lights, so landed to find out
where he was. His astonishment, when his own

mechanics ran out to grab the wing-tip flares, was tremendous. Some guys are lucky, fancy landing at your own aerodrome when you're lost. He just handed his report in and passed the test with honours. I expected he'd go missing one night, but not just at the time when he owed me a hundred francs—just my luck! To crown all, everyone's leave was stopped, and considering I was next to go, it came as a bit of a shock.

Soon after this, we moved back to our old home at Ochey and settled down to a spell of good weather, in consequence of which shows were numerous. We roamed away over Hunland, night after night, sometimes two or three times before daylight, and some of the trips were hard ones at that. Everywhere the enemy had considerably increased his defence. There were 'Archie' batteries and machine guns, and the approach of a plane was the signal for some spectacular displays.

We had a narrow escape one night whilst raiding Thionville. The machine gun fire was pretty hot, and I knew that some of it must have been too close to be healthy, although I did not realise this fully until next morning, while overhauling my machine. I found then that the centre strut was shot through, the bullet having apparently passed within not more than six inches of my head. There were no less than eight bullet holes in the wings, and between Thionville and Metz we had encountered about seventeen searchlights. It had needed some manœuvring.

The same night, Williamson and Penruddocks

went missing and the Hun dropped a note a few days after to say they were O.K. After our next show, Kirk and Richards were also reported missing. We were raiding the Kreuzwald Power Station and surmised that the enemy had bagged two more victims. Imagine our amazement when, three days later, they walked into the mess in French uniform. Theirs was a great experience: they landed in a quarry in Hunland and Richards was knocked unconscious. The night was dark, so in one way they had something to be thankful for. Richards recovered after a while, and they were able to make off in a south-westerly direction. In the darkness they had stumbled headlong into a gun emplacement, and with great daring and presence of mind, they managed to crawl away, running whenever they could until they came on a communication trench. Discarding their flying clothes, they scrambled through barbed wire entanglements, and then, hearing Germans talking, were obliged to lie low for a bit. Dawn broke, to find them on the edge of 'No Man's Land.' They laid there all day, suffering much discomfort from hunger and thirst. They could see enemy shells bursting in the direction of the French lines, and made their plans, moving at dark until they came to the Moselle River with its barbed wire entanglements. Here they were challenged and fired on by sentries, but took cover for a while, and then found a narrow part of the river. This confronted them with the difficulty of crossing, and Kirk was not a good swimmer. As they expected more entanglements to be in the river, Richards went across first to see if all was O.K. He then returned and followed Kirk across, by which time they were nearly perished with the cold and tried hurrying to warm themselves up a bit. More wire impeded their progress, however, and they were forced to take cover a good many times, repeated shots being fired in their direction. Eventually they discerned C Lighthouse in the distance and knew they were nearing safety. They had so often flown over it, but never thought to find themselves walking to it from the enemy lines. A little later they encountered French troops, and after changing into dry clothes, were taken to French headquarters, had their identity proved and were finally allowed to return to the Squadron. For this effort, they were mentioned in despatches.

Metz was the next target, and Brown and A. M. Johnson both went west. The enemy were getting too accurate for our liking and it meant keeping a little higher for safety at night.

Shortly after this, our Brigade Commander paid the Squadron a visit; came to congratulate us upon the successful raids we had carried out. We thought it an excellent opportunity for reminding him that some of us had had no leave for some time, and he promised to look into the matter and see what could be done.

For his especial benefit, we turned out bright and early that night and paid another visit to Metz. The night was good, and as A Flight was leading, with ourselves flying second machines, I thought we would try out a new stunt, and instead of approaching the town from the S.E. we would go on past for a while, then turn and come in over from the north.

We went on undisturbed until just to the east of Metz, between the town and the Forêt de Remilly. We knew this wood well—shaped like a letter T, it was very familiar and showed plainly on the darkest night. It was also the hiding-place of several anti-aircraft batteries and machine guns, and we always gave it a wide berth. The enemy had apparently become wise to the fact that we always passed between this forest and Metz, for on this particular night we were suddenly confronted with three powerful searchlights, placed in the form of a triangle and working with their beams together, forming an apex. We wondered what had struck us when they first appeared, and Bourney, my observer on this night, who was new to the game, was tickled to death. He signalled to me that he wanted to have a pop at them. We were at five thousand five hundred feet; I pulled the joy stick over, and kicking the rudder, swung round on the one nearest Metz. The other two shut down and we slipped out of the beam, taking up a position to open fire. They picked us up again, and just as Bourney was about to open up, the familiar 'woof' of a bursting 'Archie' made the plane quiver. It had burst under the left wing and was unpleasantly near. Then two more shells burst within a few yards of us and the searchlights still held us. It was getting too hot, they'd hit us

for sure if we didn't get out of that beam. Shells
by the dozen seemed bursting all over the place
and I yelled out to Bourney to hold tight, pushed
the stick forward and the heavily-laden plane literally trembled with the strain of the high speed put
upon her. The searchlight was a sticker and followed
us, there seemed no getting out of that beam.
Pulling the stick back, the machine zoomed up a
couple of hundred feet, finishing in a climbing turn
and eventually dodging the light. Bourney leaned
over and shouted:

"Cheeky beggar that, like to give him one."

"Right O!" I yelled. "Be slick about it," but
immediately we turned, he swung the beam towards
us. He was not quite so lucky this time, however
for we were dead over him and he didn't pick us
up. Bourney pulled the release and let go a twenty
pound Cooper bomb from the right under wing.
We watched, no burst, and I switched my torch on
to the bomb rack, to find that no bomb had
dropped. The rack and the left carrier were both
full.

"Try number two," I shouted to Bourney, and
we came over the searchlight again and let go.
There was a tremendous flash and then all was
dark; must have been a good shot and blown the
thing to smithereens we thought. Our patience had
been rewarded.

We made on northwards to Metz, and to our left
there was nothing but darkness, not a light to be
seen anywhere. At Thionville, we saw that things
were well lit and we were fascinated. What a

target! We continued towards it, and then, as though one hand controlled all the lights in the town, they went out, and darkness reigned on both sides.

About ten miles north of Metz, we turned due south and came straight in over the town at four thousand feet. We knew the position of the station, and throttling the engine down, we lowered to two thousand eight hundred and were over our target. Away went four bombs in quick succession, bursting one after the other, and away to the left of the main rails, we took up a good position for our big bomb. Searchlights, darting here and there, were very busy, but somehow missed us. Bourney waved me. I levelled the plane up and away went two hundred and thirty pounds of explosives in a good burst. Some flaming onions came near, Archie was busy, and other machines were around apparently, for we could see their bombs bursting. Turning south once more, we let go the remaining three, although we could only see two of them burst. Pulling away from our target we found that the near bomb on the left rack had failed to drop. Bourney tried it again and again, but without avail. He realised the danger of landing with a bomb that had failed to leave the rack and that the jerk of the machine when touching earth would be just sufficient to send it off. Poor old Scuds had met his death through the same thing.

Telling me to keep the machine steady, Bourney climbed out of the nacelle in the darkness on to the lower plane and laying flat, he released the bomb from the rack and calmly climbed back. A false step would have meant Bourney's exit from this world, but it was all in a night's work to him. Back in the mess, I shouted him a spot for a plucky effort, and he made me promise not to tell the boys— he was no glory seeker.

The German report of this raid is appended here:—

"At 8.45 p.m. five bombs were dropped. No. 86 track destroyed, several other lines rendered unserviceable, rolling stock seriously damaged. Bombs were also dropped on the railway workshops."

Night flying under War conditions is a nerve-racking, strenuous game. We had been going strong for some time, over Hunland nearly always twice in one night, being potted at from every direction, and the strain was beginning to tell on many of us. To make matters worse, the enemy had discovered our camouflaged aerodrome in the woods and did his best on every fine night to make things uncomfortable for us.

New pilots arriving about this time realised that it was a real War, while the old stagers tried their level best not to show any effects of giving way. One could always note, however, the anxiety with which operation orders were awaited each day, and the weather report would be studied time after time. The worst part was the waiting about before the show, when pilots and observers would congregate at their hangars at dusk, often not receiving orders to 'take off' for an hour or so. The weather might be doubtful, in which case we'd patrol to and fro, lighting endless cigarettes. Once in the air we were all right, but the damned hanging about got on our nerves, and we'd be all ears, listening perhaps for the drone of a Hun machine, when there would be a general scattering and a few unpleasant moments.

On one occasion, we were actually in our machines, with engines running, when the Hun dropped his first bomb. A pilot not long out was next to me, and knowing his terror of the enemy raiders, I glanced over. His machine was there, with the engine running, but no pilot to be seen. I switched off and yelled out to him, receiving his reply from somewhere over in the wood, where I afterwards found him, flat on his tummy in a ditch. It was pathetic to watch him, yet the same lad in the air and over Hunland had put up some of the finest shows in the Squadron.

The ground officers' jobs on these nights were not enviable. The French gave us more anti-aircraft guns, and machine guns were placed at spots of vantage. More searchlights were installed, one of which the Huns got first night. The Sergeant in charge was operating and received a scrap of bomb straight through his tin hat, killing him on the spot.

In addition to this, machines were missing frequently, and although reference to them was

seldom made, the thought was often in our minds,
"Who would be next?"   Great changes were
rapidly taking place, many new faces were seen
and familiar ones were absent. A machine would
crash, perhaps to-day, and the same man would
crash again in a week, and then be sent home for
a spell. Our C.O. was transferred to England,
and the new Major, well known, many of us
having served under him on Home Defence, was a
man of great understanding and knew how to
handle men. He noticed the strain that was telling
on us and immediately set to work in an endeavour
to make life more bearable. He organised trips,
arranged games, medicine ball being the favourite,
and we often went over to see the Americans at
the Chateau. They put on a game of baseball for
us and treated us right royally, their canteen being
an especial source of enjoyment and their port flips
things to be remembered with relish. We made
many friends among them.

The birthplace of Joan of Arc at Domremy was
also visited, a quaint little French domicile with the
coat of arms and figure over the entrance. On
'dud' nights, we'd go into Toul or Nancy, have a
good feed and then go round to see the girls. They
were always pleased to welcome 'les Anglais Aviators, plenty money.' Old Madame Lefroy would
pull the slide along to see who was there, her fat,
greasy old face would beam, and with the request
of 'une minute,' she would dash off and clear out
the 'locals,' making us, in consequence, mighty unpopular with some of them.

Number nine, with the red lamp, was a dingy-looking hole, the meeting room, as we called it, reeking of cheap scents and powders. The floor was bare for dancing and over in the corner was an antiquated piano, minus a few ivory-tipped keys, the rest having a nasty habit of continually sticking down. Crofty used to produce some nasty discords on it. The walls revelled in a display of tall, short, fat and lean nude females, and underneath each, scrappy quotations written in many hands. Madame would see us all with a drink, clap her hands and in would stream the mademoiselles. This parade always amused us, especially the piece of tulle draped diagonally across, plus shoes and stockings. Why the attempt to hide? They might just as well have been like the pictures on the wall. Dix, who had been a shop-walker before joining up, insisted on the parade being carried out properly and wanted them in one at a time, the same as mannequins. The piano stool was placed in the centre of the room and each female mounted in turn and posed as Venus, one of us revolving the stool in order to allow the audience to pass comments, favourably or otherwise.

There was Marguerite, the little tubby one, who looked great. Fifi, the tall, dark one, also the favourite; another with a very flat nose like a boxer and whom we nicknamed 'Pug,' and then a very big girl with fat legs. Johnny used to call her 'Tiny.' They were some girls, with a happy knack of making you buy cheap champagne at a big price, which helped to swell their commission. They enjoyed our visits and we were out to have a good time. Fun ran high and we spent a lot of money, which was all that mattered to them. Nevertheless, they often got very annoyed when, after perhaps about an hour, we got fed up and disgusted with the whole show, and departed.

CHAPTER IX

LEAVE

ALTHOUGH the fact that no leave was being granted made us rather down in the dumps, we felt a decided benefit from the efforts of our new C.O. to give us some recreation.

The enemy was pushing hard and gaining much ground in the direction of Paris. Our forces were concentrating on the Marne and our American friends were ordered into the line to receive their baptism of enemy fire. We went over there to say "Good-bye" and wish them the best of luck. They were as keen as they could be, although few of them had the least idea of what was before them; a good job too perhaps, and they acquitted themselves creditably in spite of it. The pick of America's manhood, with their splendid physique, they made a great sight when they marched off. We never saw them again.

The night of the Americans' departure from Neuf Chateau, one of their countrymen, a Major attached to the French Squadron over at Toul aerodrome, thought he'd like to see what night flying was like. He accordingly hopped off in a small scout and flew straight into the Mount St.

Michel on the outskirts of Toul, smashing everything up, including himself. He apparently forgot
all about the hills.

One of the Handleys, belonging to 216 Squadron,
landed on top of the forest away up near the line,
and made a remarkable hit; no one was hurt and
the machine stayed just where she was put. The
crew climbed down trees and found a new way of
arriving back from a raid.

The French Squadron at our aerodrome lost a
number of machines, and then, on another occasion,
the enemy hit one of their hangars and put a few
more out of commission. The Huns were using
Gothas now, twin engine machines, which carried
good loads and could do long shows. He started
to visit Paris, the French got the 'wind up' and
asked us if we would concentrate on the aerodromes
from which these new machines were leaving. Our
secret agents were not long in finding out the necessary information and great preparations were made
for carrying out the destruction of these enemy aerodromes and machines.

We were all at the hangars one morning, it was
raining 'cats and dogs,' when the Adjutant arrived
with great news. Leave was started and I was
lucky enough to be able to go off at once. Gee!
can you imagine how I felt? At first we thought
he was joking, it seemed too good to be true, but
no, it was right enough, and in my excitement I
threw my hat up and did a Maori Haka. I felt
like a man reprieved; ten days in Blighty; Hell!
what a time I'd have. It took me about two ticks

to get my traps together and I lined up at the orderly room for my leave warrant. Green eyes gazed at me from all directions, and I had commissions from the boys sufficient to keep me busy for about two days. I was to go round to Alf Dunhills and get at least a dozen pipes, all shapes and sizes, with the white spot. Perk called me aside and confidentially whispered a request that I would pop in and see his girl at the theatre. She was in 'The Bing Boys.' Of course I would. "Don't mention number nine," was his final request. Siddley gave me a letter. "If you have time, will you deliver it?" he wanted to know. "Tell the wife I'm O.K.," he said, "and have a good look at my nipper, and tell me what he's like when you come back. I haven't seen him for a year. Tell him Dad's soon coming home." When I returned, Siddley had gone west; the kid was a bonny boy, but he never saw his Dad again.

It was not until the afternoon that a tender was available to carry me to the station. The rain continued and the boys asked permission to accompany me into Nancy. I knew what that meant and I wasn't wrong; it was some night. The train for Paris did not leave until six-thirty a.m., so on arrival in Nancy we set to, bent on enjoyment, making straight for the 'Estaminet' for a good feed. Fourteen of us soon cleared the plates of hors d'œuvres, and we tried every French dish, including snails and frogs' legs. We ate from seven-thirty until ten p.m., and to finish up with, I offered to shout cigars all round. The box was

passed and when it came to settling up, it had
disappeared. We hunted the whole show for it,
but without avail, and I had to shell out for the
lot. When we got round to No. 9, I found that
Cherry, who was tight, had pinched it. But I was
going on leave and nothing mattered.

Fun ran high at Madame Lefroy's. Bill and
Dix were in great form. The usual parade took
place and then a concert, at which everyone had to
give an item of some sort, if it was only a smutty
story. I think the latter items predominated. Pasy
disrobed down to his under-pants and did the
sword dance with a pair of carvers. He was
encored loudly and then gave us 'The Dying Swan,'
after which Cherry did a few tableaux, assisted by
two of the damsels. Kelly lined up the empty
champagne bottles on top of the piano and started a
cock shy business. Anyone knocking off two at
once with an apple had to shout. Half the bottles
were in pieces on the floor when Dix succeeded in
his attempt and gave his shout, and then we lined
them up again, the girls becoming excited and
Madame very rude. Some of the girls, on business
bent, started a little diplomacy, and one by one the
boys disappeared, until in the end there was only
Johnny and myself left. The mademoiselles with
us got very annoyed and told us we were no damn
good. We gave them five francs each and then
they loved us again, "Tres bon les Anglais Aviators." I told Fifi that I was going to England to
see little English girl, but she only turned up her
nose and remarked:

"English girl cold like ice, me very warm."

Soon after midnight, we collected the mob together, had a final drink, and Madame, with her pocket full of francs and all smiles, ushered us out into the narrow cobbled streets. Some of us stumbled in the darkness, because it was dark, and others stumbled for other reasons. Scarcely had the door been closed on us, when a shot rang out and we heard it ping distinctly as it passed. We all ducked and made for cover, two more shots were fired and we beat it round to the Hotel L'Angleterre. We discovered later that some of the 'locals,' who Madame had chucked out on our arrival at No. 9, had frothed for revenge and had patiently awaited our departure, risking their shots at us under cover of the darkness. After this, we gave No. 9 a wide berth for some time.

On reaching the hotel, Johnny insisted that they all come in for a farewell spot, and poor old Monsieur landlord was wakened from his slumber and made to serve thirsty aviators. I remember seeing eight bottles come in and a misty picture of someone lying on the floor with someone else applying chunks of ice to the forehead, and the next I recollect was being rudely awakened and told it was five-thirty a.m. I was in a beautifully cosy bed, all by myself too, and turning over, I settled down once more. Again I was rudely awakened, but this time it was accompanied by a bowl of hot coffee and rolls, with the reminder that my train went at six-thirty. Then I remembered, of course I was on leave, and looking round, found a note

pinned to my tunic, 'Don't overlay; have a good
time,' signed by 'The Mob.' Some of the signa-
tures were priceless too. Well, my leave hadn't
started too badly, so hopping out of bed, I prepared
to dress. I found, however, that sleeping in one's
clothes has the advantage that one only had boots,
Sam Browne and cap to put on. One boot was
under the bed, while the other was in the chamber,
a very limp looking affair, and they looked mighty
odd when at last I got into them. The Sam
Browne had completely disappeared, so I had to
keep a British warm on all the time until I got to
London.

The Channel trip was long and tiring, and
feeling a real cot case, I settled down in a corner
for forty winks. Then, a hefty bang on the back,
and I was looking up at Chicko, boasting three pips
and a flight in one of the crack Scout Squadrons.
Several of our old cadet pals had gone west, he
informed me, Nichols, Franks, Spinky, Tony,
Roberts, Mumms, Sheather and Davis. Chicko
had been lucky, although he'd gone to pieces and
was going home for a spell. I wondered often
enough myself how long I'd be able to carry on;
the dread of the nights coming, the waiting about
before the shows and the enemy's bombing. At
times I felt it getting me down; why couldn't a
man get a Blighty and slip out of it for a bit; something would happen sooner or later, nearly all the
old boys had gone, but it was just a matter of
carrying on, I supposed.

Chicko and I parted at Victoria Station; it was

my first time on leave from France, and the scene that greeted me at the station often haunts me still. The sea of faces at the barrier as the men trooped along the platform, every eye concentrated, trying to catch a glimpse of some dear one, a son, a father, a brother, a husband, many of them home for the last time, men whose sentences had only been postponed, back home for a few precious days. It was not New Zealand and there was no one to meet me. Nevertheless, the scene fascinated me and I watched some of the re-unions with interest. A bit of a boy in front of me was trying to run with his heavy load of equipment, the mud of the trenches still clinging to him. He scanned the faces of the crowd as he passed until, a little ahead, he saw a poorly-dressed elderly woman, frantically waving both arms. "Jim," she tried to shout in a muffled voice. He rushed to her, and as I passed I saw them kiss. There were big tears in her eyes and the poor woman muttered, "Jim Boy." There were lots of mothers waiting near the two who had just met, one a very old lady, bent with age, whose sight had apparently failed. She was standing patiently with a younger woman and three children, and they were trying to point out the object of their search.

"Yes! there he is, Mother," the younger woman said, "can't you see him?" "Tom!" she shouted. The children's faces were lit up with joy, as they yelled in chorus, "Dad." The man spotted them and hurrying over, kissed first the old lady, then the younger woman, then each of the kiddies in turn, taking the baby into his arms, and the happy group moved off.

A young nurse was standing alone at the end of the platform; she showed no trace of excitement. A young officer, not more than twenty and wearing the M.C., approached her. She smiled, they kissed, and taking his arm, they made for a bus. I noted that she wore a wedding ring.

Good old London was just as busy as ever, held just the same atmosphere, the only note of difference being that everyone seemed to be in uniform, the men in particular and a good many of the women too.

Sauntering out of the station, I made straight for my old rendezvous, the Strand Palace Hotel. Gosh, it was good to be back again in civilisation; a bath and a feed and I felt brand new. I next got busy on the telephone, ringing up a few old friends, receiving invitations and I was set. After dinner, I went round and dug out Perk's girl, had to bribe the bird at the stage door to get to the dressing-rooms, where I found her. She was some damsel too; Perk's taste was good. She was busy making up, so gave me a date. The following night she came to dinner, and I gave her all the news about her beloved Perk, afterwards picking her up at the end of the show. She dragged out the whole bally chorus to introduce to me, and eventually we landed at her flat. I felt a bit of an ass with all those dashing females around. I was all right in men's company and could manage one girl at a time, but not a whole musical comedy

chorus. At any rate, we carried on until somewhere around three o'clock in the morning, when
the party broke up. I had a devil of a job getting
a taxi and then drove all over London dropping
chorus beauties. The last one hung it out and we
saw daylight on the doorstep.

Later in the same day, walking down the Strand,
I met Inky and Wigley, the latter all decked out
with D.F.C.'s, bars, and goodness knows what else,
looked like a General at least, and with his arm in
a sling. After potting fifteen Huns, one got him
and he came down in flames, but got away with it.
He reckoned that S.E. 5's were the best he'd flown.
Inky was on Bristols, got out of night flying, liked
the daylight better. He was home for good, had
a bad crash. He said his motto from then onwards
was 'Two feet firmly placed on the ground.' He
managed it too, bagged a staff job at Adastral
House.

Next morning I had to pay Father Cox a visit.
For some unknown reason, he'd credited me with
two children's allowances, then finding his error,
had debited me with the cash advanced. Unfortunately I'd spent it, with the result that there was
an overdraft. There were a large number of
doubtful-looking ladies lined up at the counter,
cheques in hand, presents from gentlemen friends,
and a good deal of tittering went on while I tried
to explain to the teller that it wasn't my fault they
had added two children's allowances to mine. He
referred me to the manager, who said that there
was another pilot with the same name and it was

he who was responsible for the two children. The whole thing, unfortunately, was an error, he said, to which I replied:

"Well, in future don't credit me with being the father of his children, not that I mind the cash, it's the taking back of it that I don't like." The error was not repeated, however, and in the end I had to cable the chief for a loan to reduce the overdraft. He sent it and fifty pounds more, but I never had a chance to spend it in London then, for on my return to the hotel I found a wire awaiting me. Opening it, I read:—"Return at once. O.C. 100 Squadron." I knew things were pretty serious in France, but I never dreamt of being recalled. It was hard to believe. I read the wire again and again, but it only had one meaning; return to that hell I'd managed to get away from for a few days.

I wasn't windy, yet there was something I couldn't explain. I'd been lucky, but it couldn't go on, night after night, something would happen for sure. It had happened to Taylor, LeFeurve, Collins, Ford, Scuds, Andy Reid and Willie. Nearly all the old boys had been lucky for a while, then their turn had come. Most of them have got a white cross now; I supposed there was one for me and it was better for a man to get it over there than anywhere else. But if it had to be, I wanted to go down white; some chaps turned yellow, but it wasn't their faults, poor devils. Stuffing the wire into my pocket, I automatically walked to the bar and had a good stiff whisky. One wasn't enough, so I took another, then two or three more, and walking out of the bar, the light seemed bad and I nearly knocked another Flying Corps chappie over. He wanted to know where the hell I was going. I had a good look at him; his voice seemed familiar; it was my old pal, Brooky. Of all the people in the world, he was the best to have for company on my last night in Blighty.

Brooky hadn't altered much, still had the pink and white complexion of youth—'Mother's fair-haired, blue-eyed boy.' The only thing I noticed was that he seemed taller and literally towered above me, and I'm only just under six feet myself.

We took up a position at the bar to exchange news. "What Squadron are you with, Bow?" he inquired.

"Same one," I told him.

"We heard that nearly all the old boys in your outfit had gone west," he remarked, with a tone of surprise at finding me still alive.

"Not far wrong," I informed him. "We have runs of bad luck. What about yourself; where are you?"

"Oh, we shifted from St. Omer down to the Somme way; hot shop too; only short shows, but plenty of 'em. I'm just home for Home Establishment," he said, with a feeling of security.

"Well, I'm off back in the morning, been recalled; hard luck, eh?" I said, and suggested we had another spot.

We yarned away and he told me that Robby, Jefferies, Stoney, Alf and Hughie were all killed.

Jack Earle, Cromie and Harte were smashed up but still alive, probably only to spend the rest of their days in bed. I told him to shut up, I'd got to go back to it. So we pushed off to Daly's and spent the evening. Bed did not see much of us that night, at two a.m. we were sitting in the lounge, still yarning, and smoking cigarettes by the packet. At six a.m. when the greater part of London was sleeping, I packed my kit and came down for a bit of breakfast. The cleaners were busy washing the floors, chairs were turned upside down and the carpets were up. I poked my head out of the door and saw a nasty, grey, foggy morning, with a misty rain falling, the whole scene in keeping with my feelings. I shut the door and made for the breakfast room, where I found five or six other officers, evidently also going back. I tried to eat, but a cup of tea and a roll was all I could manage. I had no appetite. At six-thirty I went up and said "Cheerio" to Brooky. Lucky devil, I envied him, he was pretty safe. Still, he'd done his bit. He wished me luck and "Keep your pecker up, Bow," he shouted, as I closed the door.

Seven a.m., Victoria Station, cold, dismal, the same crowds, only so different. Thank God I had no one to say "Good-bye" to me. I hated farewells. Red Caps were busy, hurrying poor devils of 'Tommies' into the carriages; "Good-byes" everywhere. Here a boy was being almost dragged out of a woman's arms by a Red Cap and pushed through the barrier on to the platform. The train is full now, men in khaki at all the doors and windows. A bell rings, the train begins to move, handkerchiefs are waved, a last "Good-bye" is shouted, and as the train disappears, the crowd moves off, here and there a lone figure, lingering to the last, waving a final farewell, and then turning to go back to the humdrum of everyday existence, while the one in the train, knowing what is before him, curses the army, the War and everything in general One of a soldier's few privileges, to curse and growl.

In a seat, in the front of the train, I settled down and tried to read, but a few pages made me tired of it. The chappie sitting next to me wanted to talk, insisted on talking in fact, and I didn't want to. I wanted to think; in a couple of nights I'd be back in the air over Hunland; I couldn't get my mind off that; could I stick it out? That was the one question I kept asking myself, but 'Kismet' would decide.

CHAPTER X

AERODROME STRAFING

THE enemy was making a desperate effort to reach Paris, and had got as far as the Chateau Thierry, giving the Parisians a very anxious time. The raiders came every fine night, and often at about two o'clock in the afternoon, Big Bertha sent over her message of hate. The day we passed through, that is, another pilot, whom I had met from 55 Squadron and who had also been recalled, with myself, the first shell landed fair and square on the Gare du Nord at two-ten p.m., doing much damage and causing a general scattering of railway officials. The population of Paris had the 'wind up,' and I never saw busy streets empty so quickly. An interval of roughly fifteen minutes and a second shell landed on the banks of the Seine, hurling masonry high into the air and leaving a huge gap in the parapet of the building. A third shell found its way to the outskirts of the city, and fortunately on this day there was no loss of life, although a hundred or more souls were reported killed on a previous occasion, when a shell landed in the Eglise St. Gervais. We went and had a look at the damaged building and saw that the roof had collapsed with the explosion, falling in on the congregation. No wonder the morale of these highly-strung people was broken. Already many were wondering how soon they would be forced to leave their homes and seek shelter elsewhere.

To reach our squadron, we had to go a long, roundabout way, the main line, which ran through Chateau Thierry, being then occupied by the Huns. It meant a long detour, and the C.O. was interested to know how I arrived back safely and which way I came. Apparently, a few days previously, a train containing bombs and supplies of spare parts for our Squadron, not to mention tail skids, of which there had been a breaking epidemic, had been captured by the enemy. The unfortunate driver, not knowing of the Huns' swift advance, had driven straight on into their territory—rather a rude awakening!

At the Squadron, things were much the same as when I left. The nights had been mostly fine and a good deal of flying had been in progress. The Squadron roster had changed accordingly. Chambers had stopped a Hun bullet coming home one night and was perhaps then back in Blighty. Some of the boys said "Lucky devil." Duncan had rejoined his old unit and been killed, while Haley, Matthews and Brotherhood had gone over to 55 Squadron to give a hand. They'd all gone down, missing, believed killed. Lockhart, one of our old boys, had been killed up at Trezeanes. Reinforcements, to fill the vacant places were expected any day. 55 had been having a bad spin, losing

machines day after day, but they never wavered.
Time and time again, the same men who came back
at dusk, went over again next morning, doing great
shows against tremendous odds. They were flying
D.H.4's and really needed escorts, for the Hun
scouts gave them a bad time. For the first show
after my return, our target was Boulay Aerodrome.
I wonder how many people, reading the announce-
ment of a raid such as this, had any idea of what
actually took place.

"Last night an enemy aerodrome was success-
fully attacked by our bombing machines."

Headings of this description appeared in the press
so much, that they became quite commonplace,
reading as an official record, dull and uninteresting.
Yet to those taking part, it meant life or death,
and excitement ran high.

Boulay Aerodrome will always be remembered
by pilots and observers who figured in the many
raids carried out by them. It was the home of the
Gothas and Friedrichshafens, used by the enemy for
his night work, and although these machines carried
out many raids, we never allowed them to get the
upper hand. Systematic attacks were made by us
and several of the enemy machines were destroyed
when landing, pilots bringing their machines down
to low altitudes to drop their bombs. Sometimes
the Hun arranged to land at emergency places, and
we often had roving commissions. Immediately a
light of any description showed itself, one of our

machines would be hovering near enough to investigate, and as the unfortunate enemy came to land, a little present from above would descend, and if not actually hitting him, would be sufficiently near to give him a nasty shake up.

On the night of June twenty-fifth, fifteen machines left the aerodrome to bomb this target for the first time. From C Lighthouse, it was roughly fifty miles north-west and took us about two and a half hours. Everyone seemed to be in a happy mood on this particular night and it promised a good show. As a matter of fact, Crofts celebrated his twentieth birthday, hence the jovial spirits.

Darby, the gloomy one, with Keely, our comedian, as good contrasts, went off in great style, declaring that there would be no Boulay when they came back. Keely never went without his mascot, a gruesome-looking animal, while Darby always carried a piece of some tartan.

About five miles from the line, my engine gave a bit of trouble, the valves sticking. It was risky to go on, so we turned back and had to take out another plane. Just as we taxied round into the flare path for the second time, the Huns dropped their first bomb on our aerodrome, about two hundred yards to the right of us. The flares were immediately put out and we took off in the dark. Getting away from the aerodrome, we climbed to one thousand feet and hung about, hoping that the enemy might lead us to his haven. We saw four of his bombs explode, and although he hit nothing of great importance, his aims were better than usual. We turned and made for the line. The lights on the instrument board continually went out, and as only two of them were luminous, it proved a great nuisance. In the end, Bourney hung over from the front seat and held the joy stick while I fixed it.

The array of instruments on the old Fees numbered ten to a dozen and often wanted a good deal of watching, the oil pressure in particular continually giving us trouble. The engine on this bus was noted for over reving, so they tipped the propeller blades with brass and the extra weight corrected it O.K. We purred along at twelve hundred in high spirits, one or two impudent searchlights looking round for us, but we missed them all this night until, when some ten miles from the target, two rather persistent streams caused us a lot of worry. In the end, we had to shut them up with a few rounds from the Lewis.

We had no difficulty in finding the target. Ours was the last machine, and long before we got there, we could see bombs bursting. There were no end of searchlights, all busy, to say nothing of 'Archie' and machine guns. In fact, we began to feel sorry for ourselves, knowing what to expect.

We could easily distinguish the two rows of hangars and a fire was burning half-way down the longer row on the eastern side; it was going strong too and proved a good guide for us.

Coming over at two thousand feet, we had a thorough perusal and darted off northwards just

as they were opening up at us. Turning back, I
throttled down a bit, and yelled to Bourney to be
ready to let go. The target showed up well and he
was good on the mark, letting two drop. We
waited for the bursts and there was only the
fraction of a second between them. They were in
a dead line with the fire, slightly in front, and
pulling away to survey, we found to our delight,
that our hits had started another fire quite close to
the first.

Bourney was very elated, and as he leant over
to me, I could see by the glow of the instrument
lights that his face was lit with a grin of satisfaction.

"Go back and we'll give 'em the rest," he
shouted. This time we came in from the east and
a searchlight caught us just as we were in a position to let go. The release was pulled and away
went another bomb. The searchlight still held us
and the machine gun fire was coming up on all
sides. Side-slipping was of no avail, he stuck to
us like glue and we were anxious to let go the rest
of our pills on the right spot, more particularly our
two hundred and thirty pounder. I tried a dodge,
and let go the parachute flare; the ruse worked, for
as soon as the flare lit up, the searchlight left us
and concentrated on the light drifting away in the
wind. We immediately levelled up, took position,
and let go our remaining five bombs, their little
propellers spinning away, screeching their warning
to those below. The two hundred and thirty
pounder gave a terrific burst, falling among some

buildings. As a parting shot, Bourney gave a few bursts with the machine gun—"For that persistent devil on the searchlight," he said.

Taking up our homeward course, we had only left our target a few minutes when Bourney spotted what appeared to be landing lights, away to the left. He called my attention and we turned to investigate. They certainly were landing lights, but we could see no sign of a machine. Perhaps one was about to land. I throttled back to silence the engine as much as possible, we had plenty of height in hand, while Bourney, all on edge, was ready at the gun. Then, as though specially for our benefit, a twin engine machine came into view, we were right above, and he was landing with the lights full on him. What a sight! He ran, stopped, turned round and taxied back towards the lights and then stopped again, right in the glare. We saw tiny figures running out to him. What a target, and no bombs. We immediately dived and let go a whole drum. We were not more than six hundred feet and the tiny figures scattered like magic, the lights instantly went out and all was darkness. There was no challenge from below, nothing happened, Bourney shot off his last few rounds and we made for C Lighthouse, having had the best bit of fun for many a raid. We told our story in the mess later, and Cherry declared we always had all the luck, although his turn came a few nights afterwards.

One hundred and seven bombs were dropped on or around Boulay Aerodrome on this our first visit, and fifteen machines returned safely. A good night's work.

The German report read:—"Civilians stated considerable damage done. Four hangars east end of aerodrome burnt out."

During the War period, pilots often got very attached to their own particular plane, and by noon of the day, following a raid, the hangars would present a busy scene. Riggers would examine machines for any bullet or shrapnel holes, or find any adjustments to be made to the rigging, and perhaps, at the same time, mechanics would give the engines a thorough overhaul and fill up with benzine, oil and water ready for the coming night. Bombs were never put on until just before the commencement of a raid. The Flight Sergeant would report O.K. and the pilot would then take his machine up for testing, the fitter or rigger usually accompanying him. Knowing they might be called upon to fly with the pilot, made the mechanics more careful in their work, although on the whole, we found them very conscientious and complaints were seldom made. On the contrary, there was a feeling of true comradeship throughout the Squadron, the 'esprit du corps' was great and everyone hoped the other would do well and thereby keep up the reputation of the Squadron.

On the morning after the first Boulay raid, Bourney and I strolled up to the hangar as usual, to have a look over the machine we'd flown. I was not surprised to find several bullet holes, one within a couple of inches of the elevator hinge.

Most of the machines had been hit, but none, fortunately, in vital spots. There must have been hundreds of rounds fired off at us that night, the enemy apparently having a good supply of machine guns. It was almost impossible not to get hit somewhere, tracer bullets in particular not being spared.

Baron Von Richtofen, the crack Hun airman, in his book, "Der Rote Kampfflieger,"* referring to raids carried out by our Squadron on his aerodrome, writes:—

"I will not divulge the number of machine guns, but there were enough to go round when the Englishmen came on the second night. We each dashed to a machine gun, and a few good shots among the other ranks were similarly armed, the rest having rifles. The pursuit flight was, at all events, armed to the teeth. The first machine came very high, as on the preceding night, and then came down to fifty metres, coming straight for our quarters, much to our delight. He was caught in a searchlight beam and was not more than three hundred metres from us. The first man opened fire on him and all the others followed suit. A storming attack could not have been better beaten off than this attack by a single impertinent airman at a height of fifty metres. He was received by a murderous fire. He could not hear the machine gun firing, of course, owing to the noise of his engine, but

* " The Red Air Fighter."

he saw the flashes and must have been a
jolly good man, for he kept straight on his
course. He flew directly over us, we naturally
made a rush for the dug-out, and as soon as he
was away, back we ran to the guns and at him
again. During the night, the fun recommenced
several times. I was in bed when one of the
Englishmen flew so low over my habitation that
in my fright I pulled the blanket over my head.
The next minute I heard an incredible bang
outside my window. I rushed out in my shirt in
order to fire a few shots after him. They were
firing from everywhere . . ."

Up against gun fire such as this, it is little wonder
that bullet holes were often found in our machines
and that many went missing.

At lunch on this day, the sole topic of conver-
sation was the coming night's show. Operation
orders were not up, but we presumed that it would
be the same target. Darby maintained that it was
not necessary to go again, he'd already blown the
place to smithereens, and Keely backed him up.
Cherry wanted badly to go; he had visions of
Gothas landing in brilliantly lit flare paths specially
for his benefit, while Johnny reckoned that it was
his turn.

Our mess was pleasantly situated in the woods
and it was now summer. After lunch, some would
retire to their favourite corner either to read or
write, but the steps leading up into the mess was
where most of us gathered and talked. Miles

would light up his cherished cigar, Bright Eyes would puff away at a very much smoked cherry wood pipe, while the rest of us enjoyed gaspers and passed caustic remarks about the smell of his old two bob pipe. The pipe suited him though, for he was as lean as a barber's pole and a great one to laugh, although all his laughing never made him fat; he was too full of energy for that, always doing something.

The mail usually arrived in the afternoon, and was the signal for whoops of joy, after which quietness would reign, until letters were read, then there would be an exchange of news, after which everyone would walk up to the orderly room to see if operation orders were posted up. Eager eyes would read with interest the orders for the night and comment on them. They were always pinned up next to the raid roster, a card designed by our orderly room Sergeant, on which each pilot's and observer's name was written. After each raid, a stroke was placed against the names of those who had taken part. There was great competition between many to see who could get the most strokes. Newcomers, keen as mustard, would gaze at the long row of strokes after many of the names, with envy, hoping to see their own so adorned before long. On this occasion, we were right in our assumption, for Boulay proved to be the target again.

The nights were very short at this time of the year and we seldom took off until nine-thirty or ten o'clock, giving us scarcely time to get in two shows before daybreak. Any old Fee not well on his own side of the line by dawn, would have been a certain victim for some early-rising Hun scout. We took good care not to be caught that way though.

This second raid on Boulay was a night of thrills, for no less than three Gothas were seen landing and were promptly bombed, the last being set on fire. Cherry, much to his disgust, missed the bus, while Johnny came back full of it. He could hardly wait, before getting out of his machine, to tell someone. At supper he held the floor and described the whole thing. Like a hawk hovering over its prey, so he hovered over that enemy machine, then, as a bird would dive at the right moment, so he had dived, flattened out and let go two bombs. He saw them burst almost on the machine and then the whole thing shot up into a mass of flames. It was still burning when he last looked back. After this, everyone was most anxious to take part in these aerodrome raids, but all didn't get the same thrill that a few of us had been lucky enough to have.

We paid them another visit on the following night, and two more hangars were set on fire. Their aerodrome must have presented a well-shelled and battered appearance, for no less than two hundred and twenty bombs had been dropped during these three raids. The fact that they did not retaliate bore out our assumption, and photographs, taken by the Day Squadron, verified our reports, to say nothing of our secret agents' reports, which came through periodically. We all felt that we had done good work and Paris was allowed to enjoy its nights again, if only for a brief period.

I wonder if the reader can imagine the feelings of an airman who, having been shot down by the enemy, crashes in the darkness in hostile country, and as he stands there, by his own wrecked plane, hears the cheerful sound of his fellow countrymen returning.

This was the experience of Street and MacRae: the rudder controls shot away, the machine got out of control and was caught in a balloon barrage. The crash followed, Street was knocked unconscious and on coming to his senses found himself half in and half out of the plane. The machine was on its side, with one wing vertical in the air, the other crushed beneath him, and the whole on the edge of a wood. As the observer helped him to his feet, the familiar drone of a purring one hundred and sixty Beardmore engine was heard, the machine passed over them in the darkness followed by another. They both gazed into the night, knowing just about where the machines were. Street waved and muttered to himself, "Cheerio, old bean!" and MacRae gazed at the entangled mass beside them and said, "Lucky devils."

Escape, however, was their primary object, but before they had left their useless machine, a rifle cracked out, accompanied by a challenge in German. They were instantly surrounded by half a dozen of the enemy and taken prisoners in no gentle manner. Pushed into a guard-room, they found a lot of grinning Huns continually passing to have a look at them, just as though they were some curios. An hour of this and then arrived several over-dressed be-ribboned officials, one of whom was an interpreter, and a string of questions began.

"What Squadron do you belong to?"

"Where have you been to-night?"

"What type of machine are you flying?"

"What bombs are you carrying?"

The questions were hurled at them one after the other, but the only reply they could give was:

"We refuse to answer any questions."

"I suppose you know your own business best," retorted their questioner, "but you are very foolish and will be sorry. To-morrow the Commandant of Luxemburg will interview you and then you will answer questions." With this, they were roughly pushed into a motor car and taken to the civilian jail at Esche. After a bloodhound had been allowed to have a good sniff at them, they were searched and placed in separate cells, damp and cold, no light of any description and with a damp, musty smell which is familiar with the underground prisons.

It was just about this time that several of us were having a final look in the direction of the line, hoping to catch a glimpse of lights belonging to the missing machine. In silence we went to our respective huts and turned in to comfortable beds, while poor old Street and MacRae curled up on hard boards, shivering with cold, prisoners of War.

These two plucky men were subjected to much

harsh treatment. The following morning, without food or drink, they were taken back to their crashed machine and there made to pose for photographs, in many different positions. The whole of the civil population had gathered to look at them, they spat at them and would have mobbed them but for the guard. Again they were questioned and threatened with starvation unless they answered, but still they refused.

Then a German aviator tried some very clever ruses. He spoke perfect English and walked around the machine with them, commenting and comparing the smashed plane with their Gothas. He endeavoured to obtain the necessary information that way, but failed. Then two enemy airmen would start an argument about the plane and call on Street to settle the point. Again they were unsuccessful, and in the end they gave it up and the prisoners were driven to Diedenhofen.

This town was one of our many targets and had been bombed often by the unfortunate prisoners. Again the guard had much trouble with the civil population, who, MacRae said, would have torn them to pieces. Taken again to the civilian jail, they received their first food, bread and coffee. They were, by now, absolutely famished, and made a dive for the food. They tried to eat, but the dirty, greasy black bread stuck in their throats and it was more than they could do to swallow it. The coffee turned out to be acorn water.

The same night was bitterly cold, and in the early hours of the morning they wakened, frozen, their limbs so cramped they could hardly move, and their hunger intense. Again the following day, they were moved, this time by train, and at the station they were subjected to much jeering from the Germans. On this occasion, their guard was not a bad sort, he bought them some food and changed their English money with German.

That night they found themselves in Metz, and their next halt was the German Flying Corps Headquarters. Here they were treated as officers and invited to drink and partake of dinner, which they did not refuse. After the meal, cocktails were handed round and then came more questions. Always on their guard, they were prepared. Their hosts were three young pilots who spoke perfect English. They put the commencement of their questions in a roundabout way and then came to the point and asked Street straight out all about his Squadron. Street could always hold his own, and taking the bull by the horns, he put it to them:

"Now you fellows, I'm going to ask you to change places with us. If you were prisoners in the Britishers' hands and were to be questioned to death, how much would you tell?" He won. They looked at one another for a moment, then the elder one said:

"I guess you're right. We won't bother you any more Have another drink?"

Thinking their questions were finished, these two weary men were then taken to the Commandant's billet, where more traps to get information were revealed. He showed them a photograph of their aerodrome at Ochey, and concealing their feelings with difficulty, they handed him back the print without comment.

"Well," said he, "I suppose you fellows would like us to drop a message over the lines to let your people know that you are still alive?"

"Yes, we would," answered MacRae, "will you do it?"

"Certainly," replied the Commandant, "here's pen and paper." MacRae accordingly addressed a letter home, sealed it up and handed it to him.

"Where shall I drop it?" the German wanted to know.

"Oh, anywhere behind the lines."

"We cannot do that, it would never get home," said the Commandant.

"Very well," said MacRae, "tear it up, they can wait."

The German had been cunning, working on the feelings of these two men's people at home, but he failed to secure the least little bit of information and grew tired of the battle of wits which seemed so useless. He had them removed, several other stunts were tried, but they failed every time, and they eventually gave it up as a bad job.

Four days later, in a half-starved and unclean condition, they walked into Karlsruhe prison camp, where they were confined till the end of hostilities. They returned to England early in 1919, both broken in health. MacRae never regained his former self and two years later he rejoined many of his comrades of those raiding nights, over the Great Divide.

CHAPTER XI

'ARCHIE' GETS US

THE first man to go on leave single and come back married, was Johnny; cunning old beggar, a dark horse, he never breathed a word. He'd been driving niggers away in the tea plantations of India all his life, so we made an excuse for him, although he didn't get out of the celebrations on the first 'dud' night. Mimms, O.C., eats, put on a great feed—soup, bully beef 'a la hash,' followed by lamb and mint sauce. We doubted the lamb from the outset and we weren't far wrong, for it turned out to be a very old mutton which he'd bought from old Monsieur of the Mill in Ochey. The inhabitants told us that it had run the streets of the village since some of them were infants. However, the tinned peas and the pears were not bad. Nuts and fruit were put on as a special, and Johnny had to respond to the toast of the newly-wed.

Now the first night of his honeymoon proved embarrassing, for he found that he'd left his pyjamas behind. He said that his wife was a respectable girl and everyone yelled "No." At any rate, out of consideration for her tender feelings, he left the bedroom while she disrobed, and groped his way down a dark, winding stairway. They were on a motoring tour and were spending this memorable night at one of those pokey 'Inns' of the English countryside. He strolled up and down the road for a few minutes, everyone had retired and no lights were allowed because of raids, then after a while, he returned in darkness to the inn and groped his way back up the stairs. At the top there was a sort of passage with bedrooms leading off.

"I knew my wife was in one of these rooms," said Johnny, "but whether I could find the right one in the darkness was another question. I wasn't a bit sure which was the right room, but anyhow I entered the one I thought and said, 'Asleep, dear?' Then something jumped out of bed with a hell of a yell and rushed out of the room, leaving me standing there in amazement. My first thought," went on Johnny, "was wrong room, and before I could get out I was confronted by three people. One was a female in a flannel nightshirt with hair in curlers, a real scream. She gabbled away, while the landlord, with candle in hand, tried to get a word in, but she insisted upon unfolding her story, that this brute of a young man had entered her room and was going to get into her bed." Johnny told her that she flattered herself, which only started her off again. After a good deal of explanation, however, Johnny managed to convince them that he had merely made a mistake and gone into the wrong room. The female was not taking any more chances, so leaving Johnny and the landlord, she returned to her room once again, and the rusty lock of the door as she turned the key gave quite a groan.

"Eventually," Johnny said, "I found the right room, and there was my bride almost in tears at my long absence. I told her my story, but she seemed to doubt me, and then I had to set to and try to convince her that it was just a mistake. I found her more difficult than the landlord, but I didn't leave the room until daylight," he finished up, so we accepted his story and asked no questions.

After the speech, Rene, our French interpreter, whose corporation was much nearer the table than his face, Miles, Johnny, Crofts and I, bagged the favourite corner for poker, where we played until two a.m. Then Miles made himself mighty unpopular by getting fours twice, Rene nearly wept, stakes were high and each time he clicked full houses. Miles collected and shouted fizz, then someone reckoned that Johnny should certainly shout—more fizz. Crofts suggested another hand, and eventually we collected up the chips just as dawn broke.

Rumours had been current that we should soon be shifted from Ochey, and that we were to say farewell to the old Fees, which were to be replaced with Handley Pages. This was indeed great news and we were full of expectancy, although it was some time before it came true.

About this time, Dicky had a narrow escape. He was taking off on a test flight when his under-carriage came off. We did not know whether he was aware of it or not, so 'Windy' went up with the intention of trying to intimate to him what had happened. Dicky thought he was having a bit of fun chasing him and wouldn't let him get anywhere near. They put up a good show stunting between them. Windy leant out of his bus, pointing frantically to the place where Dicky's under-carriage should have been, but Dicky went merrily on and took no notice. In the end Windy gave it up and landed, Dicky following suit, the rest of us watching anxiously, wondering what was going to happen, and expecting the worst. He came in in the ordinary way, made a perfect landing about six feet up, then the bus dropped, plonk, a perfect pancake and sat there O.K. Dicky got a hell of a shock and wondered what had happened; it looked darned funny to see him step out on to the earth instead of climbing down. The owner of a camera asked him to hold the picture; it was priceless.

Following this, one of the hangars caught fire and we all had shots at being firemen, anything for a change.

Two days later, Cary got a shock in starting his machine up. She back-fired and burst into flames, and I've never seen a fellow get out of a plane quicker, except when thrown out. Considering the pilot's seat was on top of the main benzine tank, I think he was very sensible. We squirted fire extinguishers at it, but it seemed to burn all the more, so we let her rip. No one was sorry, it was a dud machine.

Sammy, Edwards and Lunghie, old observers, were all tickled to death that afternoon by the fact that they got their tickets for home to train as pilots. We farewelled them in Nancy that night. Very few of the old boys were left now and there were many new faces, Blakemore, Erwin, Ebney, Potter, Gower and Van Schaack being some of the latest arrivals. They soon got down to things. Van hailed from the States, and like all his fellow countrymen we had met, he was very keen, and made good.

The Frenchmen had a nasty crash, one of their Breguets nose diving from five hundred feet and burying itself well into the ground, catching fire. It fell just behind one of our hangars and we helped to put it out and find the remains of the two men. They were charred beyond recognition.

Heavy rains about this time made it impossible for 55 Squadron to get off their aerodrome with a load of bombs, owing to its soft, sticky surface, so each fine morning they flew over, loaded up, and left from our ground. Consequently we got to know them very well, and exchange visits promoted good fellowship and much fun.

One particularly bad day, they drove over by car and put in the time with us. The following morning it was discovered that our mascot, 'Blackie,' the dog, was missing. Someone suggested that 55 might have pinched it, so three of us set forth to rescue her. They were away on a show when we arrived, but the Adjutant, who wasn't flying, invited us over to the mess for a spot, and there, curled up on an old settee, was 'Blackie,' the object of our trip. No one said a word, but while two of us kept the Adjutant chatting, Rogers smuggled 'Blackie' over to his machine and left. The rest of us eventually said goodbye, leaving a message for the boys to the effect that the mascot had been recaptured. After this, there was quite a friendly feud between the Squadrons, the dog being captured and recaptured many times and in all manner of ways. It travelled in D.H.4's, Fees, Handley Pages, French Breguets, by Crossley car, in suit-cases and in the arms of a female impersonator. In the end, poor Blackie, who always chased each machine off the aerodrome and met them on their return, was cut to pieces through getting in the way of a propeller. She was mourned by both Squadrons, No. 55 sending us a very clever card.

The summer of 1918 was nearing its end, and with the coming of the longer nights, more raids were carried out and many of greater distance.

One of the Squadron's most successful bombing raids was that which took place on the night of July 16-17, when the Steel Works at Hagendingen were attacked. No less than sixty-two bombs were dropped, and photographs taken the next day showed a direct hit on the central blowing station, the roof alongside being blown in and the work-shops of the rolling mills burnt out.

This caused a complete cessation of work at these important blast furnaces, and some considerable time elapsed before they were going again.

It was a hindrance to the enemy in many ways, for he was relying on a big output of steel from these works. The old Squadron added another leaf to its laurels, for the place was particularly well defended, and those taking part in the raid could justly be proud of their achievements.

Shortly after this, we discovered that the enemy had practically vacated his aerodrome at Boulay. Activity was shown at Morhange and Friedsdorf, so we gave our attention to these quarters.

The beginning of August gave us ideal flying nights, clear and not too dark, yet dark enough to make it more or less safe for us. Reports had been given by some of the pilots to the effect that on some of the very light nights, scout machines had been seen in the vicinity of C Lighthouse. We knew that no Allied machines were flying, so concluded that the enemy was hoping to get some of us that way. They certainly proved to be enemy scouts all right, as we found out later.

We flew for thirteen consecutive nights and some great shows were carried out. It proved a nerve-racking game and it was impossible for some of us not to show signs of the strain. There was the list of missing and killed, others had narrow escapes, crashed, or were hit by the enemy. It was while on a raid to Morhange aerodrome one night that F.E.2 B 5664 got in the way of an enemy 'Archie' shell. Bourney was in the front seat and I was waggling the joy stick. Eighteen machines left that night to give the Hun a good rally up.

Just before dusk, the last machine left the

ground, making for the line, where we hung about, circling round to gain height, while waiting for darkness to fall. It was here that Bourney caught a glimpse of an enemy scout, which verified the previous reports. Apparently he did not see us, for he just flashed past, taking no notice, but coming so near that I thought we must surely collide. My heart went twenty to the dozen, while my hair literally froze to my scalp.

"Did you see that?" Bourney yelled out to me.

"Too right," I replied, "good job he didn't spot us." We settled down again with an uncomfortable sort of feeling.

Morhange was only a short show, not more than thirty minutes over the line, and could easily be found, both by the lake and the railway, the latter running right by the aerodrome, fifteen miles southwest of Remilly Forest.

The night was clear and starlit, and as we neared our target, we could see that there was no sign of activity, so we decided to hang around for a bit to see what might happen. Slightly to our left was Remilly Forest, with its concealed batteries and machine guns, while behind us, twinkling away, could be seen our guide, C Lighthouse. It showed up well this night; I never remember seeing it for so great a distance.

As we flew about, the cool night air fanned our faces and the lack of apparent activity made it difficult to realise that we were on an errand of destruction and that there was a war in process. Up there at four thousand feet, the whole world seemed to be at peace, not even a searchlight had challenged us. What was wrong? Surely the War had not stopped. My observer suggested that everyone was having a night off. We swung round a bit and went westward. Away on the horizon we could see that things were different—a strafe was on—the whole line in the St. Michel Salient and on towards Verdun was lit up and flashes of bursting shells could be seen. Men were working hard on the guns, hurling over accessories of death, while in the trenches men awaited with dread the coming of dawn. We turned our backs on the scene and returned to the object of our mission.

The peace of the night, which had so far reigned in this sector, was suddenly broken. Some five miles or so to the right, landing lights were switched on and we immediately turned towards them. It was Morhange aerodrome and we were within only two miles when we saw a machine landing. Automatically sticking the nose of the machine down to gain speed as we neared the enemy, we pulled up just as two bombs were dropped. One of our machines must have been sitting right over the aerodrome. They were great shots, although before we could see actually what damage was done, or whether they were direct hits, the lights were extinguished and then the fireworks commenced.

Four searchlights beamed forth at once, flashing to and fro across the heavens. I wondered how many of our machines were hovering round. We could see the machine gun flashes as they peppered forth their little glow-worms, streams of tracer bullets flying up all round. There must have been twenty or thirty guns; it was a hot shop all right, and we decided to hop in and get rid of our load.

We were watching with interest the scene below us, when a searchlight in a corner of the aerodrome caught us. We took no notice and Bourney was ready to pull off. Above the roar of the engine, we heard the 'Archie's' familiar woof, near, damned near. In the reflection of the searchlight's rays, I saw Bourney look round and signal "Keep straight on." He was sighting, hand on release, when 'Archie' sent up another shell which "got us," almost a direct hit, under the left wing. The plane rocked so much that I thought we must be thrown out. Kicking the rudder over and pulling the joy stick to the left, we swung round and slipped out of the beam. The revolution indicator had dropped to nine hundred and the engine was vibrating terribly, then the thermometer suddenly shot up to its limit and I realised that the radiator had been hit. We were losing height and it seemed as though we would have to land right away. I shouted to Bourney to let go all the bombs, throw over the machine guns and ammunition, giving us a chance to keep our height. Away went the bombs, followed by the gun and its drums. The Hun must have thought we were in a hurry, and he wasn't far wrong. We headed straight for C Lighthouse.

Our height was just over three thousand and I

estimated our distance from C Lighthouse to be
about twenty miles. Could we do it? I had grave
doubts. We were slowly losing height and visions
of dreary days in prison camps flashed through my
mind. I was in a terrible perspiration and in fear
of the plane catching fire. The heat was intense
and I seemed to be sitting in an oven. The wind
screen fogged over and I couldn't see anything,
Bourney pulled the whole thing off and flung it
overboard, and by this time the altimeter had
dropped to two thousand feet. That twinkling light
seemed a little nearer, but the engine was kicking
up an unholy row and I expected it to konk out at
any moment. But no, it chugged away like a box
of nails. Poor old Bourney in the front seat must
have felt rotten, knowing we'd got to come down
and realising it was touch and go whether we could
make our own side or not. Every now and again
he popped his head over to try and get a quizz at
the dash-board. Our whole future depended on
the next few minutes. Now only nine hundred
feet—it looked hopeless and the Lighthouse was
still five or six miles off. We said our prayers and
sat tight.

About a mile over the line was an emergency
landing ground, which I hoped to make. With the
altimeter showing three hundred feet, I looked over
the side, and to my amazement we seemed to be
only a few feet up. I immediately doubted the
instrument although it certainly showed three hundred. Perhaps the country we were over was
higher than our aerodrome. The instrument had

been set at zero before we left. I looked over again and we were near the ground all right. I yelled to Bourney that we'd have to land and told him to sit tight. A light patch appeared in front of us, it looked smooth so I throttled back and held my breath, a terrible suspense gripping me. Our wheels touched earth, we ran a bit, and I thought we were safe until there was a crash, we hit something, then the whole machine turned turtle. There was a noise of snapping wood and ripping fabric, then all was quiet.

I found myself in a half-dazed condition, head downwards and entangled in a maze of wires. Struggling to find my way out, everything was dark and quiet, save for a distant flash and rumble. My first thought was, which side are we? then, where was my observer? Speaking in an undertone, I called softly:

"Where are you, Bourney?"

"Here, keep quiet," came the reply. Thank God! he was all right. I took a couple of paces in the direction of his voice and tumbled into barbed wire entanglements. Groping my way in the darkness, I found him trying to extricate himself. He'd been thrown forward into them and his hands and face were badly torn.

"We must be near the trenches," I remarked.

"The machine is in them," Bourney said in a whisper. Looking closer, I found sure enough that she was. Again I wondered which side we were. Creeping away from the trenches, we began to discuss plans as to the best method of action.

This moment meant so much to us. The silence
was ghastly, not a sound to be heard anywhere;
perhaps these were old trenches. Returning to our
wrecked machine, Bourney found a few of his
belongings, which he pocketed. He always carried
a cake of choclate and some chewing gum, and we
were mighty glad of these now. After a good deal
of fumbling about, I found my mascot, still hanging on to the dash-board with as big a grin as
ever.

Curiosity then got the upper hand and we did a
silly thing, which might have proved our undoing,
but we were so keen to know on which side we
had landed that we climbed down into the trench
and commenced investigations.

Creeping quietly along, one step at a time, we
listened, but still no noise. Bourney whispered to
me:

"They must have used these trenches in 1870."

A few yards further on, we came to a halt at
a corner, again listening, all ears, but hearing
nothing. We decided to continue for a bit and if
nothing turned up, to get out and lie low till daybreak, when we could perhaps see for certain
where we were. Advancing cautiously, we turned
the corner, our eyes becoming accustomed to the
darkness by this time. A few yards further on I
could discern the form of a man, and further still,
a few more indistinct shapes. Bourney was following close and I touched him as a warning. We
both crouched down, muscles taut. He had seen
us! A few quick steps and he was up to us before

we had time to do anything. A revolver was levelled and a challenge:

"Qui êtes vous?" The French tongue was never so welcome, and with a sigh of tremendous relief, I replied "Anglais aviators." He doubted us, we were still wearing our flying gear and might have been any nationality by appearance. So to convince him, I produced my aero club ticket, which I always carried, printed in several languages and which served to explain who I was. He signalled us to go ahead, and with revolver still levelled, he took us to a dug-out, and in the candle light we saw that our captor was wearing the uniform of a French Captain. He read the ticket here and was satisfied. Bourney, who could speak French fairly well, told the Captain of our night's adventures, to which he listened with interest.

By this time we were feeling pretty empty, so my partner, who was noted for looking after his inner man, asked if there was any food about. Our host apologised profusely for overlooking such an important matter and immediately produced several tins of eats and a plentiful supply of vin rouge. I inquired whether it was possible to let our Squadron know that we were O.K., but he told us we would have to wait until morning, when he would have us escorted to headquarters.

We chatted on for a while, then our host had to go the rounds again. The dug-out was quite comfortable, and as we were suffering from fatigue, we settled down with a feeling that this time, at any rate, our good luck had been with us.

Before leaving the dug-out on the following morning, we had a last peep at our old machine and it certainly looked a sorry spectacle, nose smashed in, under-carriage gone, both lower planes smashed. We wanted to go over and have a thorough perusal, but our friend advised us not to; it was too risky, and a couple of minutes later we knew he was right, for a shell landed not twenty yards from the wrecked plane, followed by three more in quick succession, making us dodge back to the dug-out. Our host then detailed a corporal to escort us to headquarters, and so with our best thanks, we bade him "au revoir."

It was mid-day before we were able to speak with our Squadron. They had given us up as missing and our names had gone to wing head-quarters. Just before dark we arrived back in our own quarters and the boys gave us quite a recep-tion. We had to go through all the events of the night once again. Apparently it had been a great show and two Gothas were destroyed. Cherry got one and was tickled to death. Our secret agents' reports, which reached us a few days later, were to the effect that enormous damage had been done. All our other planes arrived back safely.

Our consistent efforts to destroy these enemy aerodromes had a marked effect. We had given them no peace. No matter where a machine of theirs landed, some of our fellows would be hang-ing around, waiting to drop a bomb or two. The morale of the enemy airmen suffered in conse-quence, so much so that one night, just before our departure from Ochey, a Gotha landed, complete with crew of four men, near our landing ground. The crew calmly walked along and gave themselves up.

Questioned by our Intelligence Department, the pilot, a sergeant, stated that they had decided to do that rather than be killed. He told us that our bombing had been so effective that their aerodromes presented a very shell-battered appearance. Everything was disorganised and their casualties had been so heavy that there were very few of them left.

This was indeed gratifying, and having accomplished our task, we passed from aeroplane strafing back to reprisal raids.

CHAPTER XII

THE LAST BOMB

Our Commandant, Sir Hugh Trenchard, paid us another visit about this time and said all sorts of nice things, patted us on the back for good work, and promised us new machines as well as a new home. It bucked everyone up; flying the old 'Fees' night after night had become a pretty monotonous job, to say nothing of the risk, and it had got on our nerves.

The winter had been a severe one, making flying treacherous, and the summer, although bringing better flying conditions, had also caused much work and raids of considerable distance, raids which were carried out on slow, obsolete machines, and in many cases against great odds. The enemy had all sorts of snares and traps set for us, and it was often impossible to penetrate the defence of some of the towns raided. Yet in spite of the odds, the small band of fliers comprising the Independent Air Force carried out no less than one hundred and forty-two raids in those nine months. Fifty-seven of these were over Germany, Cologne, Stuttgart, Mannheim, Mainz and Coblenz being visited in turn by day and by night. It was little wonder then that many of these young dare-devils who came overseas to join us, full of ambition and visions of laurels, returned to Blighty after a few weeks, nervous wrecks. They were the lucky ones —dozens were still marked "Failed to return."

A month passed before our marching orders came through; it seemed so long that we were beginning to doubt if they would ever come through at all. Our new home was to be at Xaffervilliers, some miles to the east of Ochey and fifteen miles from the line, a matter of fifty minutes' flying from the neutral country of Switzerland. Joe rather liked the idea of this and remarked:

"Well, if I ever get very fed up with this bombing, I shall toddle off down to Switzerland and land there. They'll intern me and I'll be set." By coincidence he nearly did it too, although not intentionally. He got hopelessly lost one night and landed twenty miles from the frontier. Everyone agreed that it was bad luck and bad management.

The task of shifting a Squadron from one aerodrome to another is no small undertaking, when one thinks of the quantity of gear to be removed, hangars, huts, workshops, orderly room records, officers' and men's belongings, to say nothing of 'spare parts,' together with some eighty or so ground personnel to be transported.

The packing up took us a week, and on the morning of August tenth, all was ready. Lines of motor lorries left by road, while the eighteen machines took the air to fly to their new abode, mechanics in each front seat in case of engine trouble en route. The observers went by road.

The clouds were very low, necessitating flying at a low altitude of eight hundred feet. Cherry led A Flight and took the wrong turning at Vezelise. We wandered all over the show, eventually finding Xaffervilliers, where the first thing to greet us was an acrobatic 'Fee' standing on its nose in the middle of the landing ground, tail vertical. Johnny hadn't allowed for the bumps and anyway someone had to christen the new aerodrome.

The surface of this new landing ground was terrible, a real switchback. It took much labour and many steam rollers before we could land without a dozen or so bumps.

There were no signs of any new machines and our continuous inquiries did not hasten their arrival, so we dug in and carried on with the old 'lattice tails,' as Baron Richtofen named them.

We rigged up electric flares and an elaborate control platform. Each machine was given a signal letter of its own by which it could be recognised when returning from a raid. The machine signalled its letter and could not land until the answering letter was given back from the platform. This prevented half a dozen machines trying to land at once and avoided the risk of two machines crashing.

A flip around the new territory disclosed heavily wooded, undulating country, and no one looked forward to a forced landing at night. Information had been received that the enemy was strengthening his Air Forces in Alsace Lorraine, for an attempt to wipe us out by night raids, while several Scout Squadrons had come down from the north to give our day flying comrades of 55 Squadron a hot time. With this knowledge came signs of tremendous activity everywhere. Pilots and observers got busy on their machines, while the ground personnel were engaged in making dug-outs, trenches, benzine stores underground and all sorts of contrivances for protection.

Our information was certainly not without foundation, as it proved, for not a week passed when the enemy paid us a visit. Not many bombs were dropped, but he managed to get our benzine dump and made a great flare. Unfortunately, our underground store was not complete at this juncture. Anti-aircraft guns arrived by the dozen, and what with the bursting bombs and the guns, one invariably lost a bit of sleep.

There had been a lot of speculation in the Squadron as to who would be the first to return from leave wearing the new sky blue and gold dress uniform of the Royal Air Force, which was certainly more fit for a comic opera than for general use. No one had courage enough until 'Bones' turned up; he had nerve enough for anything, although his reception was not quite what he would have desired. His leave had commenced before our shift from Ochey, so that Xaffervilliers with its dug-outs and trenches was quite new to him.

For a week it had rained incessantly, so that the six foot trench around the mess, used by us to duck into when Fritz arrived, had a good deal of water in it. Bones arrived back somewhere around midnight, and fumbling along to the mess in the dark, he disappeared into the trench. The peace of the interior was disturbed by wild yells from outside, and Sawyer, grabbed a torch and proceeded to investigate, returning a minute later laughing his head off.

"Say, you chaps, come and see what I've found," he called. Whatever it was, it seemed to tickle his fancy, so we went out at his invitation, and there in the trench to the left of the door was poor old Bones, standing in a foot of muddy water and covered with slime from head to foot. Everyone roared.

"Hell of a joke," yelled Bones, "what about helping a chap out?" It wasn't until we got him out and were back inside that we spotted the comic opera outfit and then the mob went crazy. Apparently the first thing he did when he fell into the trench was to sit down, and the sight he presented was a scream. That beautiful sky blue with a sprinkling of clay mud here and there, made him appear like the true comedian in the comic opera. We begged him to keep it on until the morning, so that someone might take his photograph, but he failed to see the joke. It was like a red flag to a bull to mention trenches to Bones after that.

The Huns visited us again a couple of nights

later, unloading a number of bombs but doing no great damage. We came off much lighter than 55 and 99 Squadron (a new arrival flying D.H.9's). Their casualties were very heavy, seven machines being lost in one day. These bombing machines certainly needed scout escorts. They had no chance against fast Hun scouts and it was little short of murder to send these fellows off each day. There was never any wavering, however, not even when the casualties were heaviest. Away they went each morning, knowing full well that their chances of returning were very remote.

One afternoon, several of us flew over to see them. We taxied up to the hangars, switched off, at the same time noticing an absence of life. There were only a few machines here and there, so we hunted up the Adjutant, who told us that the boys were away on a show, at least, all that were left of the Squadron.

"They'll be back shortly," he told us, so we stayed there and awaited their return.

At the first drone of an engine, we all collected at the hangars, everyone scanning the skies to see how many machines were returning. In the distance, we could see three huddled together in a V formation, with a fourth lagging behind. No one said a word, a dead silence being preserved until they were nearly overhead. The silence was only broken when a Flight Sergeant remarked:

"That's Captain Frank leading, the other two are B Flight, wonder who the other is?"

The three machines landed and everyone

gathered round to hear the news. Ten Fokkers had pounced on them from out the clouds above and it was a real dog fight. Two of the enemy had been shot down, only to be followed by two of ours, while a third burst into flames and went down out of control.

Who's the other machine coming in, Sir?" asked the Flight Sergeant.

"Lieut. Hall," the Captain replied. "He got the two Huns. His observer is shot—get a stretcher ready."

Hall made a perfect landing and taxied up to where we were all standing. Captain Frank gave him a handshake and congratulated him, while the men with the stretcher gently lifted the huddled body from the back seat, covered it with the Union Jack and carried it away. Everyone stood to attention in unbroken silence, until Miles suggested that we "got away."

That same night, Van Schaack and King failed to return and two more names were added to our list of missing. Destiny ordained that these men were not to return, and again we asked ourselves the question, "Whose turn next?"

Two men, riders in an aeroplane, go off full of life and zeal, ready for a raid, and in a second the whole picture changes. The machine or the man is hit, the plane falls to earth, perhaps in flames, hurrying into Eternity those two youthful riders. It happened every day, yet still these boys went on, never wavering. War is war.

Soon after this, two Handley Pages arrived.

No one knew they were coming, they just arrived, and great excitement prevailed. There were more to come, and the Squadron was at once reconstructed as a Handley Page Squadron, with two flights of five machines each. We said "Good-bye" to the first of our good old friends, the 'Fees,' two being transferred to the depot. The Handley Page pilots stayed a few days, to give us a bit of instruction.

These buses, with two three hundred and seventy-five H.P. Rolls-Royce engines, were a very different proposition to fly, heavy on controls, and it was like driving a motor lorry after a Baby Austin, although we soon became accustomed to them and everyone went solo without any crashes. The machines carried a crew of three, the pilot and two observers, one acting as gunner in the front cockpit, the other observer usually attending to the maps and bombs. Sixteen one hundred and twelve pound bombs were carried in a small cabin known as the engine room, where they hung, sliding down a kind of tube when released.

We were very happy with our new machines. The balance of the consignment arrived in due course and we looked forward to some good shows. Ere long, however, our happiness was marred by a terrible tragedy before we had ever done a show with our new machines.

Little Box, the bantam, and a very popular pilot, together with 'Inches,' who, with Box, had recently been awarded the D.F.C., and Boyd in the front seat, left for their first show in a new plane, full of life and thoughts of great doings. They took off over the control tower, while those on the ground gave them a cheer and wished them luck, when suddenly the machine stalled and fell to earth like a stone, bursting into flames. A full load of benzine made it impossible to get near. Bombs exploded and everyone had to scatter, helpless to do anything for those three lads trapped in a blazing inferno.

The loss of these three capable and popular officers was deeply felt by all, and we were again reminded that it might be our turn next.

For a few days afterwards, everyone was very quiet. These crashes always cast a gloom over the Squadron, but we soon forgot—one had to. New arrivals came along and took their places. The old hands were very few now, eight or ten at the most; they would soon all be gone. Some just flew away, while others went like dear old Box. At any rate, it was all for one cause.

Starting on short shows first, we got going with the Handleys. All the boys declared them "Great," but "devils" to handle when the searchlights were busy. They wouldn't side-slip and manœuvre like the old 'Fees.'

Joss, a new observer, was in his element with those sixteen bombs hanging in the engine room, and would pop in about every five minutes to see if they were O.K. He gloried in destruction, his only growl being that there wasn't enough. His face always betrayed disgust when the last one went, and he wasn't satisfied unless he could let go all his .303. He would fire a whole drum at one searchlight, and if it didn't switch off, he would give it another. When everything was gone, he would sit down in misery for the remainder of the trip.

For a while, we had a run of good luck, plenty of flying and no casualties.   Several pilots had reported that they were sure the enemy had scouts up at night, one crew even reporting that they had been fired on from above while being held by a searchlight. The presence of mysterious coloured signals from the ground was also noted. Everyone got a bit on edge and wondered what this new stunt was; it was anything but pleasant to be potted at by scouts, and these Handleys presented a target big enough for the average scout not to miss. Perhaps, after all, we were better off with the old 'lattice tails.'

No new machine had arrived at the Squadron to take the place of the crashed plane, and it meant that we were one short. Eventually, two of us were sent up to an aerodrome outside Arras to ferry one down, and while we were away, had the great pleasure of seeing one of our scout machines do to a Gotha what the enemy was trying to do to us.

It must be remembered that we were a separate unit, apart from the army, away down in the Vosges, and had little information as to what was going on in other parts of the line.

On our way back, just before dusk, we had arrived at an aerodrome north of Amiens, where two Squadrons were operating, one flying Bristols and the other Camels. We intended staying there for the night, continuing our journey the following morning. The hospitality of the Air Force, so well known during those trying days, was extended to us, and after dinner we found ourselves enjoying a game of poker with three Americans, members of the Camel Squadron. The game carried on until about half-past eleven, things were exciting and an ace pot was in progress, when an orderly came in and informed the tall guy whom the others called 'Swift' that he was wanted in the orderly room. We dropped cards and had a spot, waiting for his return, when he blundered back into the mess, flying coat on, cap and gloves under his arm and announced:

"Some Gothas coming over—got to go up after them," and disappeared.

"That sounds exciting," I said.

"It may be, Swift put up a great show the other night," one of the others remarked.

"Let's go out and see what's doing," I said, and out we all went.

At the hangars there was great activity, but an absence of lights of any description. How these fellows managed was astounding. Three Camels were run out in no time, and our friend 'Swift' climbed into the cockpit of the first one. The engine was started, tested full out, he signalled, the chocks were pulled away, someone yelled "Good Luck," once again the engine roared full out, and in a second he was gone. He didn't seem to study the wind or anything else, he just went, disappearing into the darkness of the night.

Away to the east, the booming of guns could be heard, and the halo of light indicated the direction of the line. Ten minutes or so passed and nothing happened. Groups of men stood about the aerodrome chatting, casting occasional glances skyward, listening intently for the drone of any engine.

The first indication of anything approaching was the flashing of a searchlight some miles northward and we all gazed intently in that direction. Searchlights flashed every now and then, scanning the heavens, and a beam not two miles away from us warned us that the plane was approaching in our direction. Then the familiar drone of the Gotha twin engines could be heard.

"Wonder where Swift is?" a voice near to me muttered. The drone was now much louder, coming right towards us. Two searchlights only a short distance off lit up, scanning to and fro the sky. The drone was now right overhead, there was no mistaking these twin engines. Suddenly the beam to our left caught a glimpse of the plane and instantly the second beam flashed round, forming an apex, and there they held him at four thousand feet. Immediately a whole army of guns boomed forth, but the big silvery-looking plane flew straight on, with shells bursting all round her. The beam still held him and the firing continued, when slightly higher and behind, a tiny green light appeared. The guns instantly ceased their firing and "There's Swift," voices exclaimed. Then

above the drone of the engines, the rat-tat-tat of a
machine gun could be heard. We caught a fleeting
glimpse of the Camel as it flashed through the
beams, another burst from the gun was heard, then
a reply from the enemy plane.

"He'll get him," someone near me said; speculation was running high, everyone was excited and
bets were made. The searchlights never let that
unfortunate plane go for an instant, they did their
job well. Another rat-tat-tat followed by another
in quick succession—the big machine seemed to
rock.

"He's got him," someone yelled. Something
was wrong, it seemed to almost stop, then a burst
of flame shot out from the body of the machine,
one wing dipped, the flame grew bigger, the plane
started to fall, the nose of the machine pointing to
earth. It was diving at a terrific rate, the whole
thing enveloped in a mass of flames, down it fell,
the beams following. As the blazing machine
struck earth, there was a tremendous crash, flames
shooting high as the benzine tanks burst, illuminating the country for some distance around. No
one spoke, there was a dead silence save for the drone
of the Camel's engine.

I stood as one hypnotised, gazing at the distant
flare from the burning machine. What a glorious,
yet dreadful sight it had been—four men—enemies,
true, yet gallant—had been sent to Eternity in as
many seconds. I shuddered at the thought, for
had not the enemy been after us, trying and hoping
to despatch us in the same way. I turned away

just as the spotlight was switched on for the Camel to land. He made no circles of the aerodrome, just came straight in and landed, all done in a matter of fact sort of way, Swift hopped out, while the boys all gathered round to hear his story. The early hours of the morning still saw us sitting around in the mess yarning. Swift got the D.F.C. for this effort, and it was well earned. Camels were tricky to handle at any time, let alone at night. Flying Camels at night was little short of suicide, but it was done.

We left next morning, feeling that our trip had been worth while, and our story afforded a good deal of entertainment for the boys. Every time a visitor came along too, we had to relate what we had seen, so much so that we got sick of it in the end, and so did the boys.

Several new Squadrons arrived about this time. The enemy was apparently in for a good go and things were going to be hot. 97 Squadron turned up with Handleys, followed by eighteen Camels and a Squadron of D.H.10's. Ours was some busy aerodrome. 97 borrowed some of our observers to show them round the country at night, but the boys weren't too keen as crashes were frequent, some of the pilots being mere novices.

Many of our old pilots were sent home for a spell. Most of them had done their share and were feeling the effects of strenuous flying. A packet of decorations were sent up, Wilson, Coombs and Ross got the Distinguished Flying Cross, the French gave Miles the Croix de Guerre, Johnny was mentioned, while the rest of us still had hopes.

Autumn came along and with it the longer nights once more. Each evening at dusk, the usual procedure was gone through and the big aerodrome presented its usual scene of activity, mechanics getting machines out of hangars, while loads of bombs in trolleys were pulled up to the planes, detonators were put in and the bombs placed in their racks. Pilots and observers, with maps, would saunter up to their respective machines and carry out an examination of all the important points. After the preparatory part, we all stood by until orders were given to take the air, or if the weather was 'dud,' the 'wash-out' would be given. So September came and went, many targets were visited, and a long show to Frankfurt was put on about the middle.

It was on this show that our congenial comrade, Johnny, went missing, together with Pitman and Clainey, his observers. It was a doubtful show night and the weather had looked threatening when they left. I couldn't help wondering whether the same had happened to them as I had witnessed up at Amiens. Johnny had reported scouts and had expressed a dislike for them. That bride of his would be worrying her head off, we knew, so some of us wrote to her, trying to put a hopeful tone on the event. Great was our relief when, some time later, we heard that they were all prisoners. Apparently, one of the Rolls-Royce's failed to function; they were actually over the target, taking up position, when it stopped. Away went those sixteen bombs, the big plane was immediately turned homeward, but they were forced to land after only a few miles. Johnny put her down safely in a ploughed field, and after setting fire to the machine that had failed them, they left it to its fate and made off in the direction of the Swiss frontier. For days they managed to elude capture, existing on some biscuits and bully beef taken from the machine, but in the end, in an exhausted condition, they were forced to give themselves up.

So the enemy got their last prisoners from a famous Squadron. November eleventh arrived and our job was finished.

The first bomb dropped at night on Germany was from a 100 Squadron machine, and on that fateful night, when hostilities ceased, our machines winged their way home for the last time, leaving behind them the last bomb to be dropped on the enemy in that Great Struggle.

EPILOGUE

THE machines of War had ceased their destruction and Peace had returned to the world.

Troopships were carrying back to their native lands the men who had done their bit and been spared, some whose time had only been lengthened for a little while, others maimed for life and many broken in health.

Back in Flanders were those who "Failed to Return."

It was a Spring morning and the scene was a cemetery outside Armentieres.

A man, wearing the uniform of the Air Force, and who walked with the aid of a stick, was standing, looking down at a grave. There were fresh flowers on it and at the head was the usual white cross with its inscription.

The man stood there for some time, deep in thought, then with a shrug of his shoulders he limped away. It was his farewell to the companion of his boyhood days.

The grave was that of the school teacher, and the man with the limp was the artist.

EXTRACT FROM ANNALS OF
100 SQUADRON

During the whole of its active service career on the Western Front, no less than two hundred and thirteen raids were carried out, with a total of one hundred and eighty-five tons of bombs dropped. Approximately 450,000 rounds of machine gun ammunition was expended during these raids.

A. R. KINGSFORD

ALFRED Reginald Bellingham-Kingsford was born on 4th May, 1891, at Maidstone, Kent in England. He was the only son of dairy farmer Alfred Kingsford who died whilst "Reg" was still a child.

He was apprenticed to a photographer during his early teens, then emigrated to Australia at the age of 19, to take up a photographic appointment in Sydney. He later moved to Moree to join a friend working there as a stockman, before sailing to New Zealand to take up an offer of employment in a photographic studio in Nelson. This was where the outbreak of the First World War found him.

Reg volunteered and sailed to Egypt shortly after war was declared, enlisting in the Medical Corps - the 6th Reinforcements of the 2nd NZ Division, NZEF. Surviving the torpedoing of HMT *Marquette* he served as a corporal from 1914 to 1917, the year in which he married. In 1917 whilst in France, he transferred to the RFC, serving first in 33 Squadron then as a Lieutenant in 100 Squadron, and when peace was declared, as Instructor in 191 Squadron. His First World War activities are the subject of *Night Raiders of the Air*.

Upon his return to New Zealand in 1919 Reg purchased the Broma Studio in Nelson and followed a successful photographic career, until his retirement in 1966 at the age of 75. He and his wife, Charlotte, ("Peps") raised 4 sons. The eldest, Peter, started work with his father and on the outbreak of the Second World War, volunteered for the RNZAF. He was killed in action as a Flight Sergeant Pilot in 1942, during a bombing raid on Tobruk. During these war time years, Reg himself was "grounded" but served as Major in command of the Nelson Battalion NZ Home Guard.

Of the other sons, John, the second, joined the 2nd NZEF and was wounded in the Italian campaign. He was to become a successful architect in Hastings, New Zealand. Roger, the youngest son, died in 1947 after receipt of the Cornwall Award, the highest bravery award available to a Boy Scout. His twin brother, Hugh, left College in 1942 to take Peter's place at the photographic studio. He was appointed a Justice of the Peace, carrying on the family business until his own retirement in 1983.

Despite a very active life, Reg managed to find time not only for family, but also to enjoy the thrills of ski-ing and deerstalking in the Nelson mountains. As Founder member, later Patron, of the Nelson Aero Club, he maintained his interest in aviation, meeting and photographing such famous Aviators as Kingsford-Smith, Ulm and Jean Batten.

The appointment as a Justice of the Peace in 1940, receipt of the Queen's Coronation Medal in 1953 and the M.B.E. in 1984, rounded off many years of community service to his adopted country, New Zealand.

April, 1987, saw him "cross the line" for the last time, aged 95 years.

GREENHILL BOOKS
1988